THE BOOK OF SCENTED THINGS

THE BOOK OF
SCENTED THINGS
100 CONTEMPORARY POEMS ABOUT PERFUME

EDITED BY JEHANNE DUBROW & LINDSAY LUSBY

To THE WONDERFUL
PEOPLE AT
ARIELLE SHOSHANA —
WITH THANKS FOR MAKING
MY FIRST VISIT SO
WONDERFUL!
WARMLY,
JEHANNE

LITERARY HOUSE PRESS
WASHINGTON COLLEGE

Literary House Press
an imprint of the Rose O'Neill Literary House
at Washington College
Chestertown, Maryland
http://www.washcoll.edu/centers/lithouse/programs/the-literary-house-press.php

Series Editor: Jehanne Dubrow
Assistant Editor: Lindsay Lusby
Sales & Marketing: Owen Bailey
2014 Press Intern: Samantha Gross

Cover design by Carla Echevarria

Text set in Bell MT and ITC Avant Garde Gothic Std

Printed by 48 Hour Books, Akron, Ohio

ISBN 13: 978-0937692-21-9
ISBN 10: 0-937692-21-2
LCCN: 2013954051

ON SCENTED THINGS
INTRODUCTION BY JEHANNE DUBROW

The Book of Scented Things began, as so many books do, with an obsession. I had fallen in love with perfume, not just with the scope and variety of fragrances available in modern perfumery—roses and orange blossoms and orchids and chemical compounds never smelled in any garden—but with the bright packaging, the glass and crystal bottles, the gilded language of marketing.

I became a follower of perfume blogs with elegant, textured names like *Bois de Jasmin* and *Grain de Musc*. I read books about the art and science of the field, Chandler Burr's *The Perfect Scent* and *The Emperor of Scent*, Luca Turin's *The Secret of Scent*, and Denyse Beaulieu's *The Perfume Lover*. I learned that I was a *perfumista* or a *fumer*. I joined an invitation-only Facebook page where members discuss their "scent of the day" and exchange information about their latest purchases, finds, and passions. I discovered that experts in the art of constructing and deconstructing scent use a vocabulary that has much in common with the study of literature. They speak of perfume as if it were a narrative, a text to be read through the nose. Top notes pull us into the story, heart notes add complexity, tension, even conflict, and base notes offer resolution. And perfume, like literature, can seem formulaic when summarized; the fragrance pyramid used at every Macy's and Bloomingdale's to hawk the latest flanker of Viktor&Rolf's Flowerbomb resembles the dramatic structure most of us studied in grade school: exposition, rising action, climax, falling action, denouement.

My bathroom vanity now looked like the display counter of some out-of-the-way shop in Paris. I seemed to favor scents from small perfume companies, what are known as *niche*, not mass-produced with celebrity spokesmen, but handmade products, often with narrow audiences. My tastes in perfume mirrored my tastes in books; niche houses are the small poetry presses of the perfume world. I preferred the quiet, adventurous work of a niche brand over the latest fragrance release from a pop star, a bubble-gum eau de toilette perky with peaches, frangipani, and vanilla musk. Perhaps, as a poet accustomed to hearing rumors of the impending death of poetry, it's natural that I should root for the small, boutique perfumers, the underdogs, who are sometimes less constrained by market pressures and more able to focus on the craft of perfume-making.

Working with my friend and colleague, Lindsay Lusby (a poet herself), I came up with the idea of *The Book of Scented Things* as a way to bring together two esoteric, often misunderstood art forms. Both perfume and poetry work on the senses to create persuasive illusions, both require craft, a study of tradition, as well as a need for innovation, and both are frequently dismissed as old-fashioned or irrelevant in contemporary society.

We began by contacting American poets, writers who had published at least one collection, who might be willing to write under deadline, and who wouldn't be frightened away by the strangeness of the experiment. We were surprised to discover how many other poets already recognized the fleeting, narrative pleasures of scent. For instance, Elisa Gabbert has written columns on the subject for *Lucky Magazine* and *Open Letters Monthly*.

Jeannine Hall Gailey once managed a small perfume boutique. Moira Egan and Erin Belieu are self-described perfume nerds. Even some of those poets who had little prior knowledge or interest in fragrance, admitted that the writing project sounded weird or wild enough to be worth a try. *I'll do my best*, they told us.

Every poet who agreed to participate received an individually selected vial of perfume. We decanted fragrances into glass bottles no bigger than a thumbprint. This one would go to Jericho Brown. This one to Carmen Giménez Smith. Soon, the Rose O'Neill Literary House stank, a cacophony of twenty, thirty, forty perfumes filling all of our offices, the building more evocative of bordello than of cultural center.

Each scent we selected was meant to reflect the poet's particular aesthetic or voice or writerly obsessions. This was not science but intuition. We asked ourselves odd questions like, *If Laura Kasischke were a flower what would she smell like? What's the spice of a Matthew Zapruder line break? Is a Rachel Hadas poem an orchard or a temple?* While we believe all of the anthology's poems are able to stand alone, distinct from their scented inspirations, we've included a "matchmaking" section at the back of the book, listing the poets and the perfumes with which they were paired.

Along with a small bottle of scent, we gave each contributor these instructions: *Please, write a poem that engages with or responds to the fragrance that we have sent you.* We said the poem could be an interpretation of the scent, a memory, a series of associations, or some entirely different kind of interaction with the fragrance. We told the contributors to wear the perfume or sprinkle it on their

pillows or just sniff the scent in its glass vial—whatever
might work best for the writing process.

Months later, as poems arrived from across the coun-
try and we started organizing the anthology, certain
themes emerged: pungent *ars poeticas*, poems about the
sense of smell and the act of sniffing, poems that used
scent to meditate on the philosophical and the spiritual,
poems about the relationship between fragrance and place,
Proustian poems about childhood, poems about the musks
of the body (particularly of the female body), and finally
poems about love, desire, and the redolence of longing.
We numbered each poem in the anthology to reflect the
way that perfumers often number distinct attempts at or
versions of a scent.

In addition to the hundred poems that comprise *The Book
of Scented Things*, we also asked Alyssa Harad—memoirist,
essayist, and blogger—to write a preface to the anthology.
Harad, author of *Coming to My Senses: A Story of Perfume,
Pleasure, and an Unlikely Bride*, is not only a collector of
fragrance but she is also a trained literary scholar with
a doctoral degree in literature of witness. Her preface
makes explicit the many implicit connections between
perfume and poetry, between lovers of scent and lovers
of language.

Every poem in *The Book of Scented Things* began with a
tiny glass bottle of perfume. Many of these fragrances
came from my own collection. But Penny Lane Per-
fumes—a niche shop in Rehobeth Beach, Delaware,
which recently closed its doors—provided the project
with dozens of other samples. And, Charna Ethier, the
nose behind Providence Perfume Co., donated several

samples of her handmade, natural perfumes as well.

The Book of Scented Things was conceived of, edited, and produced at the Literary House Press, which is the publishing arm of the Rose O'Neill Literary House, a center of the arts at Washington College, on the Eastern Shore of Maryland. While the Literary House Press has a nearly 30-year history of publishing fine letterpress broadsides and books, *The Book of Scented Things* is the Press's first trade paperback. Lindsay and I oversaw all stages of the book's construction, but we also looked to Owen Bailey for help with its marketing and promotion. Samantha Gross, the 2014 Literary House Press Intern, assisted with the time-consuming process of proofing every page in the anthology. Carla Echevarria is responsible for the book's striking cover design. And, of course, *The Book of Scented Things* could not have come together without all the poets who agreed to lift those miniature bottles from their tissue paper wrappings, who unscrewed the tiny black lids, and then, who eventually found the words to name that presence, that body, that story misting in the air.

THE SCENTED WORD
PREFACE BY ALYSSA HARAD

Summer rain on hot asphalt. Gas fumes and cut grass. Chlorine. Hairspray. Cigarettes and grape bubble gum. Drying sweat. Dying leaves. Leather. The particular sticky tang of beer and worse in a dark bar at the far end of the night and then, emerging into the cold air, the pale iron smell of approaching snow.

We might not be able to name the scents that haunt us, but we know them when we smell them. No, that's wrong. We feel them before we know them, a pure gut tug of emotion that jerks us down into the undertow—the flood of the past into the present—and leaves us gasping, not just for air, but for language. "That smell," we say, disoriented, at a loss for words. "Oh god, that smell."

Even when we're not overwhelmed, scents are notoriously difficult to describe. In *A Natural History of the Senses*, Diane Ackerman points out that we have no common cultural vocabulary for describing smells the way we do for tastes, textures, sounds, and sights, no parallel for words like *sour, rough, loud,* or *bright.* But like other invisible, uncanny things, scent both resists and inspires language. Proust, whose name is synonymous with the kind of involuntary memory I've just described, found all the words he needed for his masterwork in the honeyed, blue sky summer scent of the linden blossom, or *tilleul* (often translated as "lime") tea that soaked that cookie of his. But he's hardly the only writer inspired by scent. There are even a few who aren't French.[1]

The intangibility of scent, its ghostliness, is part of its power. Both difficult to grasp and impossible to avoid, it often turns up in our stories at just the point where language fails us. We use it to signify extremes of holiness and sin: a saint dies in the odor of sanctity (roses, usually). A femme fatale—Raymond Chandler's pages reek of scent—slays with her poisonous perfume (dark animal musk or smothering white flowers, fecundity turned savage). We turn to scent when we want to talk about the pressure of forces just beyond our ken—that something fishy in Denmark—as Virginia Woolf does in *Three Guineas*, when she teases out the subtle way that gender discrimination works by investigating "the odor," "the aroma, the atmosphere, that surrounds the word 'Miss' in Whitehall." [2] (The word "Mrs.," she tells us, is "so rank" it can hardly be mentioned.) Scent can bear witness to the unspeakable: traumatic memory is the dark side of the madeleine effect—the soldier jerked back to the battlefield by a whiff of sulfur from a spent match. It becomes the haunting presence of the thing we try not to see: think of Billie Holiday, gardenias in her hair, singing "Strange Fruit": *Scent of magnolias, sweet and fresh/Then the sudden smell of burning flesh.*

But think also and always, of Molly Bloom and her Andalusian roses, singing us to the end of Joyce's *Ulysses* with affirmation after ecstatic affirmation of life and sex and risk and pleasure: *...all perfume yes and his heart was going like mad and yes I said yes I will Yes.* [3]

Seven years ago, on a hot, slow day like the one we're having as I write this, I clicked on the link to a site called *Now Smell This* and fell down a rabbit hole into a strange and lovely world of people bewitched by scent. The link took me to a blog devoted to reviewing perfume, though *reviewing* feels like too flat and critical a word to properly describe those witty, sensuous descriptions, smells unfurling one after another like scenes in a film or the chords of a song. (Music, that other invisible enchantment, is the dominant metaphor of the perfume world.) In the reviews, perfumes sparkled and shimmered. They were pink and fruity, or sharp and green. They radiated icy cold or velvety warmth. They whispered, shouted, and giggled. The problem that Ackerman had identified, the missing language of scent, had been resolved in the greediest, most expansive way imaginable—all the senses pressed into the service of smell.

I didn't care much for perfume, or so I told myself. Nevertheless, completely smitten with the trick of turning scent into words, I began following links to other blogs, reading through their archives and ordering books with titles like *The Foul and the Fragrant* and *Essence and Alchemy.* Then curiosity won out and I began to chase the scents themselves, the building blocks of a perfume vocabulary. I learned to recognize the cool touch of a gloved hand that is iris and the slap of green that is galbanum. I got drunk on the risqué funk of labdanum and the elegant raunch of civet. I spent hours reading reviews and sniffing at my scented skin, matching smells to words, until I finally understood what any dog or bee or pimply adolescent boy doused in cheap cologne could tell you, which is that scent itself is a language—one we are always trying, however imperfectly, to translate.

I never had a true Proustian moment of recovered memory in those early months of sniffing, but there was something deeply familiar about the joyful intensity of those half-secret early morning and late night hours. It was the feeling I'd had as a teenager, sneaking in very early and very late to the windowless, book-lined room where my parents kept our hulking computer to write love letters and poems and to read poetry, diving in at random to anthologies pulled from my parents' collection of old college books.

So it made a kind of magical sense when I began to see poetry on the perfume blogs. At first it was only a line or two at the head of a review, often in the original French or Spanish. Then one of the most popular bloggers began devoting the odd Sunday to poetry. Finally I stumbled across a beautifully written blog called *Memory and Desire* wholly devoted to pairing poems and perfumes. And there in the margin, underneath the word "Because" were the final, perfumed lines of Molly Bloom's soliloquy.

I wrote to the author, and we became correspondents, writing back and forth to one another several times a day. She was the first poet I befriended because of perfume, but by no means the last. I can't help speculating on why so many of the people I know who love and know a great deal about perfume also love and know a great deal about poetry. Do we have a penchant for distilled essences, in both scent and language? A love of invisible things? Are we pale, bookish types who wouldn't crave so much olfactory stimulation if we spent more time outside?

Are we merely perverse? For it has to be said that the most obvious thing poetry and perfume have in common is that so many people feel comfortable declaring that they hate them without knowing much about them. (*I, too, dislike it,* begins Marianne Moore's famous poem on the subject. She's teasing, of course, but that "too" still says everything.)

Or if we aren't perverse, perhaps we're excessively, inexcusably feminine. Poetry and perfume have enough trouble on their own, but together they become a slight pair of somethings that belong in the corner of a well-appointed boudoir on the vanity table next to a bouquet of hothouse flowers, or tumbled together in a heap with yesterday's silk stockings, a moth-eaten feather boa and a handful of crumpled, lace-trimmed valentines. (...*there are things*, Moore continues, *that are important beyond all this fiddle*.) [4]

I write those sentences and hear Muriel Rukeyser's rejoinder sounding in my head: *They fear it. They turn away, hand up, palm out/fending off moment of proof, the straight look, poem.* [5] It's a strong argument—contempt is always one degree away from fear—and one I've always believed about a certain kind of poetry and a certain kind of prose, too. And while Rukeyser certainly wasn't thinking of elevator asphyxiation or overzealous department store spritzers, when it comes to perfume there are other, deeper fears to consider: fear of announcing one's presence or being marked too strongly by another's, fear of sex and sensuality, fear of our snuffling, howling, hungry animal selves.

Perhaps it all comes down to how you feel about unexpected invitations. Perfume and poetry don't take up much space, but they are made to expand in all directions and to take us along with them when they do. They reach down into alchemy and magic. They accompany our prayers and sacrifices, and our rites of love and seduction. When we say yes to them, it's not always easy to tell where we might end up, or who we might be when we get there. *Who is this,* asks the Beloved in that most fragrant and holy of love poems, Song of Solomon, *that cometh out of the wilderness like pillars of smoke, perfumed with myrrh and frankincense, with all powders of the merchant?* Sometimes we don't want to know the answer. Sometimes we pause on the threshold. Sometimes we run to the door to find out, fingers dripping sweet-smelling myrrh on the lock.

BASENOTES

1. As you might expect of a nation obsessed with wine, cheese, chocolate, perfume and sex, French literature is particularly fragrant. Any scented word canon would be incomplete without the works of Colette (who often uses scent as a key to character and sensual revelation), Baudelaire (especially his heady *Les Fleurs du mal* and *Correspondences*), and J.K. Huysmans's *À rebours* (in which the dissipated narrator plays a fantastical scent organ whose rich chords of aroma drift out his apartment windows, subtly infecting all of Paris with the narrator's hedonism). Proust's name, and his moment with the madeleine, have become near-automatic signs for scent and memory. An experimental "camera" that samples the air around a scented object using the perfumer's technology called "headspace" is currently being developed by graduate student Amy Radcliffe at Central Saint Martins in England. It is called a Madeleine. (Wainwright, Oliver. "Scentography: the camera that records your favourite smells." *Architecture and Design Blog with Oliver Wainwright. The Guardian,* 28 Jun 2013.)

2. Woolf, Virginia. *Three Guineas.* New York: Harcourt Brace, 1938. 51-52.

3. Joyce, James. *Ulysses.* New York: Random House, 1986.

4. Moore, Marianne. "Poetry." *The Poems of Marianne Moore.* Ed. Grace Schulman. New York: Penguin Classics, 2005. 135.

5. Rukeyser, Muriel. "Reading Time: 1 Minute 26 Seconds." *The Collected Poems of Muriel Rukeyser.* Ed. Janet E. Kaufman and Anne F. Herzog. Pittsburgh: University of Pittsburgh Press, 2006. 155.

Alyssa Harad is the author of *Coming to My Senses: A Story of Perfume, Pleasure and an Unlikely Bride* (Viking, 2012). Her writing has also appeared in *O: The Oprah Magazine*, *Marie Claire*, *The Chronicle Review*, and the perfume blogs *Now Smell This* and *Perfume Smellin' Things*. She lives in Austin, Texas with her husband, three cats, one dog, and a closet full of perfume.

N° 1
AMIT MAJMUDAR

On His Reluctance to Contribute
to *The Book of Scented Things*

All attars are unutterable

                          Dare
I concoct a caption for the air

Or clothe the genie in the bottle

What use is ekphrasis if
The canvas isn't even bare
Isn't even there

A word is far too heavy for
The strongest scent to bear

I've caught a whiff of Unattainable
A whiff as well of Longing

                                  Where

In a long forgotten woman's
Long unforgettable hair

N°2
JAMES ARTHUR

On Receiving a Vial of Perfume in the Mail

After I got the envelope you sent,
marked "fragile," I started wishing I hadn't agreed
to write a poem about perfume. Like a priest
tipsy on communion wine, I carried the little cushion mailer
from room to room, before I set it down—
and weeks went by.
For Baudelaire, perfume
on a woman's naked breast was enough to suggest
boats at moor, a quay, and fruit growing into sweetness
on aromatic trees—
but for me, what fragrance
brings to mind are in-flight magazines, and the ads I stare into
when I've done the crossword
and the sudokus are too hard, and I've got
no book to read. When I unsealed the double envelope
and dabbed some perfume on my wrist, I made a list
of the associations that came to mind. *Citrus rind,*
department stores—
I thought of Provençal fragrance-makers
crushing the essence out of flowers. I gave
the perfume to my wife, who put it by the bathroom sink,
on our one crowded shelf.
Once, she reminded me
of everything. She now reminds me of herself.
The smell stayed on my skin for days.

N° 3
MATTHEW ZAPRUDER

Poem for a Vial of Nameless Perfume

Finally stranger at the end of a long season
of constant beginnings I opened at last
the letter containing tissue paper
so carefully folded around the vial you sent me.
With giant fingers I unscrewed the black
cap marveling at such jeweled industry.
The clear liquid smelled at first
like a vast tiny ballroom full of hopes
someone else's mother had
rubbing one wrist against another
in that manner reserved for distracted
excited ready to be disappointed realists
who know for a moment all dreams matter.
I bent my head to the glass jar
and knew it was the same scent worn
by the woman staring out
of the gilded framed canvas at me
yesterday at the modern museum.
She was lying on a red realistic
yet also somehow along the edges
disintegrating couch. She must have been
at the very last party before painters
discovered abstraction and started painting
the multicolored edge of this wondrous
contaminated storm cloud age we find
ourselves alone together drinking
so much information from,
while the keepers of the house
we have not elected discuss just war
and our server farms sound like the ultimate
bee colony touching ceremoniously
down on a field of magenta flowers.
And now the third and therefore
most holy time I bring it to my face,
searching for some actual connection
to any unsentient genus my nose
could bring my brain, but there

was nothing, no gentle stroke
of the orphan forehead, no memory
of summer walking along the beach
still holding a few leaves from the grove
of fig trees, only the thought
because I am actually sitting at my table
on a typewriter typing on a ghostly
anachronistic piece of paper
I will physically send you
to truly hold, a few molecules
once part of me to your ceiling
or who knows if we are both lucky
skylight will rise, and then
an electric wheelchair through
the green space inside you
from now on everyone will know
as Emerald Park will quietly carry
a dreaming young soldier,
the room will get sadder, you will be
on an island with very long night
approaching and clouds will pass
over your head and no one will ever
know what they resembled.

N° 4
PHILIP METRES

Entre Naranjos

Dear unrhymeable, you repel
my word-hoard, unharnessable

wild horse pausing beneath
the last wild apple in the last

unincorporated field
in the world. In you, Sanskrit

gardens hang. In German,
you hail from China. Persian

emperors kneel before you.
In Russian, I recall you as apple

sin. To unpeel you
from you is to be stung sudden

by sweetness. I've longed
so long for you, unrhymed, I live

in two time zones. The before
is now our after, long past

our laughter, the tower of tears.
We've been so long together

it was like we were apart. Now
it's time to wend and wind back

to the field, the tent and want
of the wind. Let me lie down

in you, unsplit, as you
devour my mouth.

6

N°5
CONNIE WANEK

A Scent

We needed a carpenter's level,
a bubble steadied on a line,
caught between verticals, perched there
like a hummingbird egg.

The job required a tool
that could tell us all was well,
briefly (and by extension, forever).

We found a tiny vial of perfume,
the very one you gave me, a few raindrops,
melted snow and roses,

and held that against everything crooked
and it worked! A perfect world
came true! Quickly then
the first nail went in.

N° 6
CODY WALKER

Pure Oud By Kilian

The best among the four oud samples I have from Kilian.
—Transmeta, Jan. 3, 2013 (basenotes.com)

*Smells like Diet Oud; I can already picture a Montale fan
wondering out loud, "Where's the oud?"*
—Diamondflame, Feb. 22, 2010 (basenotes.com)

Dude! An oud feud!
Let the salary-men take note.
Get a punch card, a chad-extractor, cast your vote:
Transmeta
or (rad name) Diamondflame.

(Me, I don't weigh in—
I'm Switzerland; just sayin'.
Kilian's killin' it. Pure Oud's plasticky,
fantasticky.)

Troll on, crazy Diamondflame!
Well met, Transmeta!
And yet, a question: Am I
not myself a Montale fan? (*Sì,
poverino*: in Galassi's English.)

Holy Selassie! I emerge from the oud
feud
renewed.
(Truth told, editors, I'd wished
for 7 Billion Hearts: its
"very fine vanilla absolutes"
bring out—in me!—the vaudevillian.
But thanks for the Kilian.)

N° 7
SANDRA BEASLEY

Banked

The letter promises "Blackberry Bay"—
a noir inlet, ripe and bottomless,
patrolled by spiny dogfish who kiss their dorsals,
candling eggs against December chill.
I expect salt on my skin, the scent
of waiting. Instead what comes is
"Blackberry & Bay." Grammar as a bowtie
to happiness: the basket full, the evening warm.
When clients came to René le Florentin
they did not know if they were getting
poison, or oil. They had to bank
social debts against the shame of a body
that smelled like a body. Five centuries later,
perfume is decoration. Except when destination.
Except when you thought I wanted to run
through a field of *Magnolia virginiana*,
while I readied to swim the dirt depths below.

N°8
MEREDITH DAVIES HADAWAY

My Cat Knocks Over the Perfume

And now my desk, alive with *apricot-jasmine-tea*,
refuses dreary tasks—the cat has dressed it up
in sticky notes and shiny tacks, paper clips dangling
from an open drawer, a smear
of Wite-Out winking. This cat's all *freesia*
and freedom. She's not just thinking *sachet*,
but away, away—*sashay*, as she glides
down the stairs—no work today. She's *translucent*,
She's *clear* and, furthermore, she's out of here.
                              Gone now,
till after dusk, strutting the streets in search
of leather and musk. *That's it*, I say in the morning.
She only rubs a scented paw behind her
ear and yawns so wide I see her missing tooth.
So much for beauty. So much for truth.

N°9
RACHEL HADAS

The Lost Bottle

Given the sweet assignment
Write about this perfume,
I open the tiny vial
and dab some on my arm.
A meadow hot with blossoms—
tropical? Caribbean?
Something that smells of sun
and that embraces dark.
Jasmine? Magnolia? Plaka.
Taverna. Early Seventies.
A copper pot of wine.
The gypsy stops at our table
with her basket of white blossoms.
The one picked out for me—
I can smell it now.
An azure veil drapes
each expansive future
now desiccated, trapped
inside a flower's ghost
which has the ghostly power
to bring what's vanished back.

Vanished: I lost the vial
or it lost itself.
Did I perhaps leave it
in the hotel in Haiti?
I thought I brought it home.
Wherever the container,
something did stow away,
invisible and weightless:
the genie memory,
recovering the promise
and pleasure of a night,
delivering the flushed
pounding heat of day.

N° 10
ROBIN EKISS

Through Smoke

No one ever called me *Petite Chérie*,
my dear little one, perfumer
who built Hadrian's Wall
by stirring roots into the dirt.

Roving amiable little soul
he said of his lover, a term
of affection, private distillation,
a degradation. *Through smoke,*

in Latin, is what perfume means.
Elegy of ash to ash: no one ever
called me *Petite Chérie*, dear little one,
in French. Some scents are subtlety,

like the goat's milk and rose petals
guests in the court of Louis Quatorze
bathed in. Pears cling to their stems,
history sours on the wrist: every amen

this far north is an amiable roving,
a raving so dear. Little ones: *a woman
who wears no perfume has no future*
and I no daughters or dead to perfume,

just this one heart in its odorless distraction,
whose pulse brings heat to the flower.
A woman dies after a pear is pulled whole
from her chest. I'm not her. Affection is artifice

and aroma, affectation and misnomer:
what little soul can I leave you, my son,
who will remember my scent, even
with this empire between us?

N° 11
SHARA LESSLEY

Scent of the Gods

All's beautiful because it's not: green-gold donkey
          scat, honeysuckle and cat
shit, pomegranates erupting burnt-

amber above the dirt park whose live-in attendant
          (Porta Potty beside a cinder-
block shed) I once saw

take a chicken by its neck and wring it into a feathered
          tornado he plucked at dusk—
I smelled its blood. All's

beautiful. Because this country's not just table grapes,
          but the olives' acidic skin,
onions ruptured in

crates strapped to jingle trucks spewing diesel and soot
          across the open air
stalls of Amman. Lotus

buds riot *jade-blue jade-blue* above scattered bird
          bones. Men hand-set
their alphabet of oils

into a wooden press: ambrosia, prickly pear,
          plant sap and styrax. *All
the perfumes of*

Arabia couldn't sweeten this bloody hand, cried Lady
          Macbeth, a pinch of hyacinth
read across her wrist.

All's beautiful? Khaled's bottled anise seed, metallic
          whiff burning cardamom
and flint. *This,*

he swears to God, *special just for you*: lemon rind

                        seared in ox fat—its oil
feels like silk. It's true

even Cleopatra bathed in asses' milk, arsenic-laced
            salve dabbed just-so
behind her ears. The scent

comes clear: musk and oud, a thirty-petalled
            kwanzan alighting in my palm.
All's calm. I pass

the vial back, am handed an alabaster bottle
            from which the city
skips unloosed—*rain*

raining piss-colored grains, electric glints pulsing
            rain and rain, *rain* at day-
break, *rain* spilling over

oil-slick traffic circles, *rain* steaming the sewage
            drains, three-thousand-year-old
underground caves,

pear-shaped drops of rain bursting the silvered
            rumor of rain, *rain* rushing
the walk-up soap shop

where strays pick at fat-scraps and gristle
            dumped by the butcher's son
into the lanes of water-

starved Amman, a balm *raining* mercury
            and mud flooding
the goat-hair tents,

the vendors' precarious towers of melon turning
            green-darker-green, sweeping
the veined globes

clean, *rain* on my face, on my lips—that scent,
            that mineral twinge
of beaded iron

stalled overhead in the palm fronds.

N° 12
JANE SATTERFIELD

Menthe Fraîche

> In conjunction with James Heeley,
> Michel de Montaigne, and Andrew Marvell

Done correctly, every scent works

& though I fail to follow

the trail of each of twenty-eight

raw materials sourced, there's

herbage here, enough

to better fit us for contemplation,

arboreal as the frosted sage

of antiqued Wedgwood Jasperware,

the mojito's icy cool.

One whiff's a stand of oak, burled

& verdigrised by rain, the patch

of mint beside the porch. Here's

hedgerows & the hush of a disused

potting shed, shards of broken

pottery, herbs spilling healing

roots—& though I haven't worn perfume

in years, here comes Remembrance

with her satin clutch, wrists dangling

with charms, precision-guided

assignations, hellos, good-byes

in rooms that reeked of Polo

& Obsession, Opium, Anaïs Anaïs—

scent a taser to the brain. *Green thought*

in a green shade, the snap of sheets

in summer wind, stolen kisses, a mossy

wall, the dank waters of the Grand

Canal & coinage of some other realm.

N° 13
NATHANIEL PERRY

Axis Mundi

We have a stand of cedar trees I cut
and use from time to time for posts or parts
of a gate or rails. And I know well the heart
color of their heartwood when I set

my wedge to work a useable seam, but still
I get surprised sometimes by the change in tone,
relearning, as we do, what I'd already known—
that darkness is usual and is what fills

most vacancies inside. There's an evergreen
in southeast Asia that, when diseased, darkens,
and its natural fragrance (which, of course, also marks
my split cedars) turns dense and strange and seems

to come from a far, difficult place, exiled
but trapped in the wood. Like everything we take,
agarwood or *oud wood* is precious, hard to fake,
component of our version of the world,

which we sometimes think that only we have made,
but there's the tree and the fungus and the perfumes
in their little bottles left on dressers in rooms
framed with pine in houses that we say

are stick-built, as if we lived in trees. Which we do,
I guess. At least I'm with them a lot, peeking
at their hearts like I said, or in the thirteen weeks
of winter, though you shouldn't burn cedar. I use

this wood as ballast, something slow to rot—
in the ground, in the rain, or in the clouds of years
they hold and help hold back like they were weirs
for wind or our exile hours, which they are not.

N° 14
EMILIA PHILLIPS

Midnight Noir

In a crowded elevator, you smell a perfume—
      too strong—& think it rude

      as dank cologne on
an airplane, hazed in the bathroom & thumbed

      along the stubbled ravine from

The Long Traveller's greasy earlobe
      to the elbow bend of

      the jaw. For whom? The question,
for naught. The unoriginable

      spume most certainly noticed

by the others. So, that's that: you're all
      smelling it, ascending

      in a box from the ground
to various departures, yours. If the mephitic exits

      first, she'll still haunt,

ectoplasmic, with her scent long
      after she leaves. Perhaps this

      is her way of remaining
after she's gone. You know this motive

      well: each poem, a nano

droplet in your oeuvre's cloying mist of *I am!*
      Only a few more seconds.

      The man next to you lifts his
glasses to wipe his eyes with a hankie,

& you think *it isn't all that*

bad, why, there's a hint of vanilla—
    the word itself perfumes

    with association. Language
only engages one sense directly—sound—

    and the others come

through memory. If someone were to
    describe the perfume

    to you, you would have to
use your whole life to conjure it. *Bergamot*

    would beget the Earl Grey

in the Styrofoam cup you had in the hospital
    caff the day your brother

    passed; and *a floral note, like*
gardenia: the Cinnamon Bay hike on your honey-

    moon where you twisted your

ankle & your new husband left you
    on the trail for being

    too weak. And the *something*
beneath, I'm not quite sure would return you

    to your mother with her cheap

vial of White Diamonds, saying she's never
    been able to discern the different

    instruments when she hears
music—all of it one sound—& your father,

    now in a forensics lab in Kandahar—

where the people your country inter
         believe the soul comes gently

         from the body as a drop
from water &, then, is perfumed by the angel

         of death with the eau

of paradise, the sweetest musk on earth—
         writing in an e-mail: *How's*

         my sweet girl?

N° 15
CATHERINE WING

Sniff

The Lipstick Rose unfurls
in a curl of pretty.
It tendrils thin about the wrist
in a vine of vapor and waft.
The weather's aflower
in a fragile bath of lace
and powder.

But success is something
meaner down the hole,
towards the bedrock cave
and surfaces that sweat.
Well knows the brave perfumer
in his lab and coat,
who atomizes the bloom.

He's strapped and yoked
to the animal that lives there,
not at the heart but core of things,
all lizard rank and smell.
It hulks rather than prances,
and the chemistry's a prison
not a room.

And when it works, the dainty
vial, the creature opens
his nictitating membrane
and—but slow—blinks
its milky lid. It's not a rose
that rises, and the shade
is blood on the lip.

N° 16
DOROTHEA LASKY

You think language is silly until it happens to you

I write you
From above an ocean

Wilted and stale flower
I used to think you were odd

Until you burst in my mouth
Like the most obvious thing

All in all I was glad I had had
Another moment in the rain with you

What is all this beauty
If you can't cast a thing beside it

It was me, I astounded everything
Even the animals almost gone in the basin

You walking towards me
In the ghostly smoke

When you took off your raincoat
It was not to keep you hungry

It was not to keep you simple
It was to keep you wet

Wet and violent flower
That I shook at the people

When I described you as an ocean
It was because I was still close to it

When I looked on you dead center
It was to remember the thing with the soft outlines

It was to remember the thing
I had grown used to forgetting

N° 17
YERRA SUGARMAN

Questions Upon Smelling Sea Salt

What rocks the rowboat

on this body of water?

What is this loneliness

nothing can repeal?

Does it extract shells

like syllables from the sea,

like vowels severed from a word?

Does it salt the water,

sift the grains onto land

and into our skin

so that we might be absolved,

amended, restored to spirit?

What disappears and reappears

through this rind of light,

slouching above the dune

to mind a heron

lost on the wet sand?

What makes the eradicable

pulse of the soft and bitter sea?

N° 18
MAUREEN THORSON

A Real Psychology

Between checking the basil
      and my e-mail,
what do I know of reverberation?

Those waves that throb without, within.

Summer's shade grows heavy with mint,
      days that wear me close,
      hot vein beneath a translucent wrist—
blue of heat, blue of flame.

Who will see it? Will bring that sea?
The monotony
      of brine,
      blue snare
of wave on shingle,
whelk's tinny echo
swollen to a bass-drum roar?

Volcanic on the balcony, seismic
in the garden, the ocean's margin lingers in me,
washed in mint and wind.

Salt stings the seaweed clean.

An ocean offered to it.
Blue as lapis. Blue as vein,
pulsing and repulsing.
Its swing-and-crush recalls me:

I am going home.

N° 19
REBECCA MORGAN FRANK

The Perfumier on the Comeback of the Scented Glove

I.

Artifice is easy: the palms leathered
with perfume are no mirror for
the gardener's hands, but mimic each
flower, bush, and tree tended.
For there is no work in beauty, as
natural as a lemon grove, an early
blossom, the greengage plum.

II.

At its start, perfume was a verb,
by its end, a noun.
As is hand what we have
and what we give. The glove
is a popular gift.

III.

They can be worn, can
cover your lover's hands so when
touching the other she blossoms
in pear, grapefruit, pruneau, bergamot—
the scent designed for you.
You would come between them
wherever they went.

IV.

If not the hand, then around
the throat, silver
pomander opening
like the wedges of an orange,
fending off the body's odors
with sandalwood, cedar
masking the cloying of decay.
Every fad has its own end.
Everything returns.

N° 20
K. A. HAYS

Prediction, *Hyacinthoides non-scripta*

Now the brook's a swell
of melt in purpled shade.
A prophecy
greens up along the bank,
puts out fists,
then nods and broods.
I'd be the bee come from beneath.
Listen, rain's slung to a bloom,
and the sun's puddled, the towhee,
spring-thin, calling Drink.
Under a sweep of creek,
all valleys, mouths, and gods to be
ball up and do. They drink.
This city bulbed under,
this city to come:
a still bell. Soon rung.

N° 21
DORE KIESSELBACH

Dry Wood

We aren't born needing to replace ourselves.
It takes a flood. It takes a death.
It takes desire, sprung,
like catastrophe, from clay.
When what's bound to
happen happens, we want
a mask that goes inside.
We wear it here and here
and *here* and our skin
grows over it the way
grass grows through
limbs of a fallen tree.

N° 22
SARAH VAP

what is this perfume: mirror curves,
ambient patterns, sona sand drawing

it isn't white shoulders it isn't oil of olay it isn't tatiana

by diane von furstenberg

it isn't white shoulders—my grandmother,

it isn't oil of olay—my mother

it isn't oil of olay behind her mirror it isn't oil of olay on me

it isn't white shoulders on me

it isn't tatiana by diane von furstenberg on my babysitter, on me

perfumes behind their mirrors   perfumes of all of my mothers

perfumes inside their mirrors   and imminently on me

it isn't tatiana by diane von furstenberg it isn't oil of olay on me:

"i see you did not eat the rooster i gave to you yesterday. that is
good. you must come back and see me every twenty-eight days"

that is why the moon every twenty-eight days

that is why grandmothers, mothers, babysitters

and imminently, me

that is why chased chicken in the sand,

that is why unbroken line around the dots

that is why being careful not to touch the dots

and why one imagines the edge of a rectangular grid

imagines the edge like a mirror

with lines hitting the mirror (like light)

and rebounding at 45°

(the limits of my language are the limits of my world

(wittgenstein))

ideally, the entire figure would be traced

without having to pick up her finger

ideally the stomach of the lion,

ideally the chased chicken in the sun

so that the entire diagram is constructed with a single curve

that does not retrace itself—ideally the stomach—

ideally the shoulders

ideally the shoulders and stomach that are on me

understand that a line could intersect itself

that a line could bend back around

a line could require the grid to change

but a line cannot not retrace itself

the line can never retrace herself until my grandmother

my mother my babysitter

on me

the limits of my language are the limits of my world

(wittgenstein)

understand we call such patterns "networks"

a "network" is a system of lines that connects points

the limits of my language are the limits of my world

(wittgenstein)

understand an "algorithm" is a recursive procedure
whereby an infinite sequence of terms can be generated
the limits of my language are the limits of my world
(wittgenstein)

the limits of my language are the limits of my world
(wittgenstein):
some designs correspond to light-ray patterns created
with the addition of horizontal mirrors between the dots
or vertical mirrors that open and close
or mirrors that reposition themselves around the grid

mirrors that bend the lines which imminently
white shoulders on me
mirrors switch the line which recursive white shoulders on me
mirrors that algorithm which switch the white shoulders on me
which infinite which requisite which—now this is oil of olay on me

understand a numerical rectangle is called "magic" if
intersecting itself on me
"magic" if for all the rows and columns the sums of the numbers
of the small squares remains equal or—bad luck,
the numerical rectangle
is not "magic" tatiana by diane von furstenberg on me
is not "magic" oil of olay on me

is not "magic" white shoulders on me

is not a magic mirror is not a magic

is not tatiana by diane von furstenberg on me?

the limits of the rectangle are the limits of the mirror if

the limits in the oil of the rectangle are also

made of light or if the loop

inside the grid is also a network and is also an algorithm

and is also on me

then, if this is not tatiana by diane von furstenberg on me

then this is definitely not tatiana

by diane von furstenberg on me

then, if the limits of my language are the limits of my world

(wittgenstein)

then the limits of my language are the limits of my world

(wittgenstein)

A Vulgate

Distance and the medicinal
dust. Is the palladium
reflective?

Beliefs notable primarily for how one
cannot retain them today yet can nevertheless
say little else. Enough
to let the weight of the book
rise to the mouth. A plane with wings so long
it never has to land.

Also, this church was named for snow that fell in August.
Burnished agate snowcloud with the threadcount
of an amaryllis. They overturn petals in the nave to honor it.
And which province has the honor of providing those petals?
And who is charged with the pleasure of overturning them?
A proportion of sail to craft that wildly outweighs,
I trust it and err toward, proportionate
breezes through the dry hives and vetch, my pliant camber,
my idiot's wreath made by removing the greenest parts.

But the best singers know only one song at a time.
The songbird, hawk-clasped, said what it always had.
Therefore,
I don't mind
if the early safety
of splintered light
comes apart in a prism of cream. It's all right.
I'm in there, and it's all reunion. Any moment now
is some other time.

N°24
MICHAEL DUMANIS

Clouds

Because I was afraid of death
I hid my body in a cloud
of vetiver and citron notes
and thought I could persist forever
as something burdening the air
of any room I had to leave.
I carved my name into a tree,
forgetting that the tree would fall.
Crossing the canvas as my paint peeled off me,
I hollered music out of my small teeth.
I thought I could outlast the weather.
Here is one room I had to leave.
Those are my diamond dust shoes in the corner.
I am a dark shape on a video monitor.

N° 25
RICK BAROT

Mystery Joins Things Together

The pupil. The cornea. The lens. The retina.
The eye is made of parts the way the world is made of parts.

The stirrup. The anvil. The hammer. The cochlea.
So with the ear, its parts like things
from a hardware store.

But mystery joins things together.

The sheet of rice paper leads to the old woman's hands,
leads to the white morning glory
twining the cyclone fence of a city lot,

leads to an abstraction about nostalgia.

Seeing the silver afternoon sea, I am not seeing the sea
but my mind leaping

to the argument I heard yesterday on the bus, then leaping
to the galleons sailing from Manila to Acapulco,
four months across the blue

expanse, with their spices and porcelain and ivory.

When I open the vial, the perfume inside
has a smell that travels to the nerves in my nostrils and then

to an orange grove in a summer dusk,
its beauty measured by the ditch that the mind wants
to keep out. And the Sprite can in the ditch.

And the canvas glove that a picker has dropped.

Mystery joins things together.
The copper beech. The shoebox with the flashlight inside it.
The poet in his overcoat, writing the lines

about his own death, in rain, in autumn, in Paris.

N°26
JAMAAL MAY

Per Fumum

     —Through Smoke

My mother became an ornithologist
when the grackle tumbled through barbecue smoke
and fell at her feet. Soon she learned
why singers cage birds; it can take weeks
to memorize a melody—
the first days lost as they mope
and warble a friendless note,
the same tone every animal memorizes
hours into breathing. It's a note
a cologne would emit if the bottle was struck
while something mystical was aligned
with something even more mystical
but farther away. My father was an astronomer
for forty minutes in a row
the first time a bus took us so far
from streetlights he could point out constellations
that may or may not have been Draco,
Orion, Aquila, or Crux.
When they faded I resented the sun's excess,
a combination of fires I couldn't smell.
The first chemist was a perfumer
whose combinations, brushed
against pulse points, were unlocked
by quickening blood. From stolen perfumes
I concocted my personal toxin.
It was no more deadly than as much water
to any creature the size of a roach. I grew suspicious
of my plate and lighter Bunsen burner,
the tiny vials accumulating in my closet.
I was a chemist for months
before I learned the difference
between poisoned and drowned.
When my bed caught fire
it smelled like a garden.

N° 27
JILL ALEXANDER ESSBAUM

Miserere Mei

Four decades
I've hoped for
a scruple of proof
to sustain my longest
longed-for truth—
that my limbic brain
isn't just some drop
and swindle shyster
swapping bundles
of probable greenbacks
for genuine lack, and
that somehow the ache
of my start-stop faith
determines that I am—
in some way—OK.
That God is God, and I,
if not exactly ironclad
good, am enough of a kind
of kindness to suffice
as *nice*. But that is not
the case.

My days are wet
and same. I wake
to pervious letdowns.
The entitlements
of coffee. The spleen
of a torn tea towel,
neurotic, if not neutral.
The phone call I regret,
the one I've not yet
placed. The iterate,
scapegrace prayer
that never veers:
God?—be there. But
kitchen petitions usually
land in the scrap bin.

With the peels
and the rinds and
the skins. For the end
of one thing isn't
always the beginning
of another.

At two a.m. the sky
is patent black and
I stand at the center
of all my mistakes.
It's winter. I am naked.
I may not be awake.
The air is vaguely
prussic, and all the bees
have left. And sleep
is the youngest brother
of death. Christ, I am
so empty that I've broken
apart a heart I didn't
even know I owned,
a second one holed up
in the ship-hold of the first
like an immigrant
indentured to a slavery
of tears. At two a.m.
the imminent rockrose
nears. I plead my mercies

here.

N° 28
JOHN GALLAHER

Avignon By Comme des Garçons

In a movie I saw once, the lovers find each other
in a sort of purgatory figured as an airport, where one
is destined for heaven and the other somewhere
else. I don't think it was hell exactly, but certainly
not heaven. There, they have a caseworker or something,
the details escape me, but there's this scene
where they're eating, and the caseworker is having something
that smells and looks (and tastes) like pâté of shit. The idea
is that to the supremely cultivated palate, there is a new panoply
of experience that we, the mere, have no access to . . .
so that the pure appears foul. We must appear unlike we are
as what we are is base. We'll be back there again,
or we'll end up there, but first let's take a tour, a celebratory
French tour. Ramparts, maybe, or Picasso's women,
either would probably work, if you're thinking of ramparts
or Picasso in the way of the Avignon Travel Guide, where
the medieval is sepia, rather than hurling feces over a wall
with a cry of "your father was a hamster and your mother
smelt of elderberry." As well, if you're thinking of exotic
and exclusive art openings, it would probably work,
but if you're thinking of the content, say some Avignon
prostitutes, you might find yourself divided. Maybe divided
is a good thing, though. Divide and conquer, etcetera,
and here's a place for seven popes to hide. "What should
a pope smell like" is probably enough to override
any lingering hope for a night on the town, but what's
in a name, anyway? I should talk, I don't even know for sure
what my name was when I was born. What should I
smell like, then? In the movie he chases her across the runway
on fire, or through fire. It's a Catholic smell, more
balmy than flowery, more bridge than water, more barrel
than wine. We've been bathing in Christmas trees.
The frankincense is undeniable. It was my favorite part
of the mass, the people in rows, everything specific,
and this smoke curling up around us. Thus sanctified,
what are we to do now? Where are we to go in such a state?
We smell like saints. We had no idea we even wanted to.

N° 29
GEORGE GREEN

Cardinal

How charming that your letter is perfumed
with *Cardinal*, the scent we shared on top
of Mount Vesuvius the night we wrote
a poem together to the rising moon.
The crater disappointed you somewhat,
but our descent was perfectly sublime.
Our guides had torches, though the moon was full,
and looked like fiends assigned to lead us down
"into the heart of hell to work in fire."
I had to compensate the devils, too.

Well, now I'm dying and you want to trill
like Cleopatra over Antony—
impossible. Wait for my funeral
and play Andromache among the jasmine
and the myrtle that aromatize my tomb.
You won't be hearing bravas from my nephews
unless you stab yourself. Their legacies,
they know, are rather paltry next to yours.

A grand endowment goes to all the nuns
at San Gregorio. And shall I lie
in state there like the late lamented princess
who under her command lay unembalmed
to nauseate the sinful and the saved?
No cardinal could cover up that stench.

I have an exquisite Batoni that
consoles me now, a Holy Family.
In truth it is a copy but I must
confess to gazing at it endlessly
while orphic warblers fill my groves with song,
and underneath your fragrant pages rests
my sacred treasury, the *Iliad.*
But why does Homer never speak, not once,
of singing birds?

            I saw a dancing girl
surrounded by the rabble at the Mola,
and pretty, really, as Batoni's Mary
she capered while a filthy urchin blew
a dented horn. It made me glad to drop
a silver ducat in her tambourine—
she nearly wept for joy; but then I saw
the scabies on her slender hand and wrist
and turned away completely disenchanted.

N° 30
ANDER MONSON

Man as Map in Retreat Seeks Brightness

I had hoped that it would curve and disappear
and take me with it, the passageway
under your city, until it did
and then I was alone down there
and all there was for me was the smell
(to say *scent* is too delicate for it), a little hell,
most of it my own, the echoes of my wounds,
my footstep sounds, end-stops from my insteps
every foot I crept, following the tunnel.

I was a creep, and worse, a scary creep,
I had been told: not man, not moth,
not mouth nor breath nor gust of wind
nor guest. Because of the incisions,
these lines that radiate from my eyes
and scar a map into the peachskin of my body,
I should shun the sun and turn
my face away from man.

I know they're disconcerting. I too wonder
at their meaning. Each night I count them
down and watch the skies for revelation.

Of course it does not come.

I bear them with what might as well be pride
but is not. At best I might have called it spite:
a refusal to be diminished by the meaninglessness
of the stars, to shrink from gaze, to count for
less. To be scarred like this
is to incur the fear response in others
and the gag response in some, Halloween excepted,
a night when I am free among the other monsters.

I learned to live with your averted eyes
& so I wore them like a Boy Scout sash,
badge-adorned, an orienteer collecting welts

on legs from scrub I refused to skirt or skip
for a reason I couldn't bring myself to name.

I should have moved.
I should have loved less.
I should have closed myself to pain
but I did not.

So I was here in the underneath
below your home, singing
into the ringing song of traffic
from above. Manholes keep
what's below the street
from coming up into the street,
you told me once, when I inquired.
I said I thought these sewers were designed
to drain the undesired away to underneath,
to keep the city livable and bright.

That was a year ago.
Now I'm here but you are not.

Occasionally
it smells of daylight and love's sliver
fading, and how spring means differently
in your desert than it does in the lake country
I once called home.

I left—well, I had been driven out
with my belongings and a strongly worded
note that told me never to return.
I could not stay gone like that
so I returned at night and festooned
the city in sequins in my stead: a burst of them
in every place I used to haunt,
a line leading into morning
to remind them of my absence:
a peacock's trail, a skunk's plume,
a sign of light and doom
for anyone who remembered me
or deigned to say my name.

I thought of the boy whose burns
I could not stop looking at

in the food court watching television:
his face polished smoother
than a lakeglass mirror. In this light
his smile became translucent. It had been
his fault, the burns, he said, the fire
he'd started in his father's workshop
after dark and how, aflame, the gases
gathered him and claimed him as their own—
but it didn't matter now that he had TV.

A new family broadcast itself to him each day,
as he flickered from mall to mall, a ghost.
He'd shadow couples—subtly, as subtly
as a bad burned shadow of a boy
can live underneath our gaze—but we were
the ones to see him there and I paused
and wondered if he was even there at all.

His fate might have been mine, I knew.
To be bound to a placeless place,
unmarked, a faceless face out there
in darkness. Somehow the tunnel smell
brought him back to mind.

An afternoon: the boy and you and I
shared a bag of lemon doughnuts
in the food court between the Sbarro
and the Auntie Anne's and the vague stink
of the trash of everyone around us
and we looked down anyone who looked at us
and did not blink until they passed
and resumed their lives. We would be
their story. We were danger,
otherness. Later they would think of us
and fuck others who looked like them
and think themselves rewarded
for their bravery.

It could have been anywhere
but it was here and it was him and you
and we were us. And then you left.

And it was just the boy and me
and the expression on his face

when I stuffed another lemon doughnut
in his mouth like a turducken and he grinned
a grin for memory. It was like he stared out
into the dark without a sense
of what it might contain
only to find it held him there
like a star along with everyone
but that somehow it was okay
because of stolen lemon doughnuts
because of sadness and Sbarro
because of pain.

I was not so sure: he was gone
so long that I knew only telling myself
this story kept him here.
Perhaps I made him up,
a golem of memory
multiplied by desire. But what else
was memory except desire
to understand a perfect afternoon?

What else was it for
if a scent from underground
could bring you back
as if you never left
as if you had not left the two of us
as if you had not left me
as if you were not now my missed
connection, maybe my only. Hit me back
if you read this and tell me what I wore
so I know it's you.

N° 31
ALAN MICHAEL PARKER

The Chair

When I came upon the man in the road
his knees drawn up   upon a little wooden chair
someone important   inscrutable   in pain
a golf course to his right   the supermarket   a gas station
a billboard tilted to the dazzled
he asked me three questions

If my memories were getting younger
If my heart were a lazy Susan
If an idea could be a perfect vial of vanilla

I had no answers   the police came
the EMT   the social workers
the friend of his sister   his sister
picked up his briefcase   his trench coat

The traffic rivered   around us   into its hurry
brake lights anxious   cell phones stared at
how beautiful his pinstripe   abandon   faith
how slow

Can an idea be a perfect vial of vanilla
stop a man
flat as the sky someday   the horizon over the strip mall
I'll know   I have his chair   I'll sit and see

N° 32
ELYSE FENTON

Mistral Patchouli

Forget sea breeze or cyclone, wind
gone Sistine on summit & troposphere.
Imagine instead infinity in a backseat Buick

driven by the ghost of my grandmother, plastic
bonnet & all automatic locks engaged. Or else
the haute petaled haunt of collared

polyester on snakeskin, afterbreath
of country kin distilled from hayloft & hammer-
down, jig & pitchfork, cows turned loose into the spare

dream of yellowed clover & the whole payload ditched
for a quarter acre of asphalt & a vinyl lawn chair
to ride out the rain carving like a broken

ramekin of sweat the body's last S curve to song—

N° 33
BRIAN BRODEUR

Barred Owls

Keening from some hollow place in their bodies, they bark
their backyard caterwauls, startling the brickwork

of row houses boarded with plywood slats. How long
can they go on interrogating in a foreign tongue,

expecting to be answered, their voices taking the shape
of the wispy ends of contrails as planes slope

out of CVG over the gray Ohio? Grainy with catkins,
the breeze smells of styrax and pine, a cheap cologne.

In the dark, they hush, stirring the garden firs,
and their silence seems to thicken the air

like words spoken in anger about the dead.
A garbage truck grunts uphill, its tires thudding

the pockmarked street, and they start to mew and hiss
their song again: *Acquit yourself, acquit yourself of this.*

N° 34
KEETJE KUIPERS

Gone South

Before the caterpillar swung to your lap
　　　from the transom, before the snake
tongued its way under your door. Before ivy
　　　undid the screens from the windows
and black rot left fleur-de-lis on your floor.

When the flowers and shoes in shop windows
　　　fattened with shadows, when the city's
black wharf lost its grin. When streetlights
　　　leaned over your path to the highway
like solemn girls who had grown too thin.

Before the possums ate all the unripened
　　　persimmons, before the pecan tree's
long fingers shed golden-lit dust. Before all
　　　the diners were closed on a Sunday
and 'bless-your-heart' replaced 'fuck' as a cuss.

N° 35
NICKY BEER

Gulf City Dialect

Here is the swamp with a hot stone lid
covering it, where the roaches are large
and buoyant as birds, and the birds coyote-sized.
The air is a solid you push through.
You want a word for the moment
after injury but before pain or pity
when you think of how lovely
blood looks on skin.
You anagram everything,
live on *Severest Own* Street,
Wetness Over Street, *Events Worse* Street.
The previous tenant left behind a box
of clipped catalog pages:
men with friendly mustaches
lounging in affordable underwear.
The graffiti on your trashcans keeps changing.
Your neighbor hides a gardenia shrub
behind a six-foot fence, but it climbs
through your open window
each night. The lizards love you,
are convinced you'll learn to read
the shapes they make on your ceiling.
Sometimes the contours of your sheets
lengthen and buckle like a receding tide,
grow legs, a sweat-thickened voice.
You seal your lips against her sex,
murmur *Maria Maria Maria Maria*
which is not her name.

N° 36
AARON BAKER

Lake Michigan

Is your dogged will blunted
by my cattish evasion? *Love* you?

As I was saying, Lake Michigan
is the only Great Lake
we don't share with Canada.
Don't you love it for that?

When Benedict Arnold was still a hero
of the Revolution, he was driven
back from the burning gates of Quebec.

The crux of the debate: breathing alters,
the crook of your knee hooked in the arc
of my narrative, your laugh, lyrical,
tangled in my measured retort.

The gates are on fire! Your ankle in my hand,
(would you let go of my hair?), the nasal
ah of your Wisc*ah*nson pressed against
the rounded *arr* of my W*arr*shington.

No, you're the one who hasn't been
listening. I like you a lot. The long water
stretches under no breeze toward shores
lit from below by the lake-light.

God bless America. A sock hangs trembling
from somebody's foot like a leaf in late autumn.

N° 37
GABRIEL SPERA

Memories of Rahway State

Joanie, the lovelorn secretary, sighed
into the phone as she fingered the slick
pages of her fashion magazine, thick
and bland as any high school yearbook, while Gus tied

his impeccable steel blue tie yet again, preparing
to meet the Violent Crimes Compensation Board
director. He was my boss, my job straightforward:
check the docket of the day's parole hearings

and pull the inmate dossiers, color-coding
the victim statements, incident reports,
the psych evals and amicus briefs, the court
transcripts and job tenders—a most soul-corroding

summer job, if not for one redeeming factor:
that bank of filing cabinets, my personal
Scheherazade, teasing out its arsenal
of hapless, greedy, flawed, and tragic actors:

- Sal, mob fall guy, serving double homicide,
  discovered his true calling with the Rahway State
  repertory, and browbeating the kids in Scared Straight.

- Rondi, possession with intent, a girl inside
  a drag queen's body, before the hormone therapy,
  self-delivered, gave him just enough to fill
  a B cup and hard nights in a private cell.

- Tomas, loaned his gun to a fellow refugee
  from a land with no word for accessory.

- Coy, model inmate, no priors, convinced his wife
  was cheating, stabbed her seven times with a steak knife
  then tried to saw her limbs off, unsuccessfully.

A grim tale in every file—given three years,
I might've read them all. But even in Rahway
time passes, and the calendar's fence of x-ed out days
meant I'd be leaving soon. But I couldn't disappear

without a flourish, without some prank or sabotage
to say farewell. So, staying late one day, I flipped
through Joanie's stack of *Elles* and *Vogues* and ripped
from perfume ads heaving with lush décolletage

the scented cardstock inserts, and gently dropped them
like ballots into random dossiers, amused
to picture the parole board, piqued and confused
to find their conference laced with Opium,

Obsession, Poison, or Eternity
while across the table, cuffed and unaware,
the subject nodded, eager, if not prepared,
to claim again the blessings of liberty.

N° 38
MATTHEW THORBURN

This Is What Manhattan Smells Like?

No, give me the steam of pork dumplings,
ten thousand made by hand each day on Mott Street,
the cool marble of Grand Central where a kajillion

people catch their trains, shoe polish and subway
ad glue and a pale dusting from the rising sun

of pizza dough spinning overhead. Mix for me
the horsey funk of hansom cabs, yellow mustard
on a hot knish, on-again off-again rain, a dash

of asphalt and taxi exhaust, the sawdust and cement
dust of buildings going up or coming down.

Give me a gust of hot bakery air, the sweet and sour
tang of a rush-hour train—newsprint and armpits,
damp wool, baby powder, a hint of hope

or disappointment, depending on the hour.
For me, it's the dark tickle of luncheonette coffee,

it's briny pickles plucked from a barrel
and the gingery waft of a Midtown sushi den.
Give me 59th Street fountain spray—faint and cool

on the breeze—from that hundred-year-old fountain
the homeless guys sneeze and dip their toes in

and even a whiff of the glossy black bags
piled high along 35th, trash shining and steaming
in the morning sun. But Corsican immortelle?

Gold saffron and sandalwood, notes
of suede? Take a hike up Fifth Ave. and spritz

some other asshole with that. Anoint my neck
and cheeks with samovar steam and the grease
of this pig floating past, roasted red and glistening,

shouldered high on a board by two skinny cooks
bickering in Cantonese and pushing through

the crowd on Canal Street. Let us sniff
mozzarepas, disco fries, decades of spilled beer
behind the piano at the Vanguard and the ghost

of cigarette smoke in all the bars you can
no longer smoke in. My city smells like milk

crates full of paperbacks for sale on the sidewalk,
like the fishmonger in her gut-mapped apron,
fish scales glittering on her wrists. It carries the zing

of pickled herring, it smells like glazed donuts
and nail polish, yellow curry, a stack of scratch-off

tickets and a dirty penny, like bodega roses, kimchi
and fried rice and the faraway ocean
smell you can sometimes smell deep in downtown

if just for a moment you stand perfectly still.

N° 39
LISA OLSTEIN

People Are Hanged Curtains Are Hung

Fruit of the vine, fish on the line
chip on the shoulder, off the old

not far from the tree. The cops
found Caesar when they broke up

the party. The landlord found Circe
when he cleared the place out.

The zoo finds tires for each
to paw and a hose to stream.

Nature says grassland-acres-ibex.
Nurture says asphalt-kibble-fence.

The sun says sleep, sleep, oh my
America, oh my newfound land.

There are three kinds of suffering
says the drive-through shaman.

I see in you a girl, a cage,
a cat, an orange-naped bird.

No, says the girl, there are three kinds
of love. Mango, she says. Mango.

N° 40
SHANE McCRAE

The Perfume

Little Brown Koko wears a wide-brimmed / Hat

in the windy country he was born to

It's easy to find God

when something's being taken from you

The black boy finds God everywhere

In the book as I remember it he hears

The voice of God in town in spring in the

morning in spring / Walking through town in spring

He smells a bright perfume / A white

woman's perfume

On the breeze it is the voice of God describing / The breeze

and even as a gust   carries his hat away / He feels

nothing he sees   nothing his eyes

Are closed he hears the voice of God

He doesn't see the white man coming

shouting with the voice of God

N° 41
NICK LANTZ

If Scent Is the Trigger of Memory, This Is What America Remembers

Texas oilmen pace the gulf,
raking beached seaweed
into great spiraling mandalas.

A B-grade slasher film opens
with a boatful of unwashed pilgrims
parked off the New England coast.

The backseat of a prominent
Manhattan limousine
writes a tell-all memoir.

The only bison a child
has ever seen appear on coins
so old the dates have worn away,

but the child rubs his thumb
over the animal's face
and whispers its name.

A national anthem
wavers across the Potomac
to a mile-long tent city,

and its closing fanfare
is the sound of a dollar bill
being stuffed into a thong.

N° 42
HILDA RAZ

Flower of Immortality, Eau de Parfum
By Kilian, $235 for 50mL

> *Shivers of flank and shoulder*
> *already drawing absence nearer*
> —Linda Bierds, "Simulacra"

We think they are delicious, these traces of freesia and peach,
evoking an utopia where people like us live apart from the world
of supermarkets and beachballs, waking at dawn
to rediscover the moon gone pale from wandering
sinking now into the mountains by our house.

On the porch is a daybed covered in chintz
where you're welcome to sleep all night
below the blazing spectacle, no gas or electric stink
to disturb stars in their patterns, striding widelegged,
waists belted, or mounted, or rocking away the end
of a journey we've been making so many years in the dark.

Or you may decide to doze away the morning, or
early afternoon, after you've smelled then devoured
a white peach martini, one of a set of three on a fan of flowers,
blossoms on the clay plate left out for you on the railing.

Or in late afternoon, your hiking boots unlaced,
poles at rest against the exquisite rose crystal lampshade
on the wicker table, the left one slowly settles
to the floorboards, the scent of white musk seeping
into your head as you sink ever closer to bouquets,
freesia in jars set by your body, bundles of organic
carrots to feed you in the coming company
of shade and philanthropy, pure loveliness, vanilla traces,
black currant, even the tonka bean, a live iris outlined in paint,
yourself gone forever, if ever hospitable,   the angels

N° 43
TYLER MILLS

Progress as Autumn Spice Dabbed onto Your Throat

Memory could open her mouth there—
how last night, all the women with brown hair were killed
on TV, each on a separate channel. How a controlled burn
forces oxygen through & through the cerulean
pearl of a wick tip of flame. My mother kept a luna moth
splay-winged in a box frame in the bathroom
next to the toilet, and you could look into the eyes
translucent in hazel skin as though they could see you—
as though they opened to birch-leaf green—
then wipe yourself, switch off the light, and leave it like that in
    the dark.
Sometimes your reward for sleeping through a football game
is another football game. And last night, people painted red
stumbled through the train—made up
like corpses of burn victims in a detective thriller,
the plot where a man and a woman, or a man and a man,
or a woman and a woman, die in a cot,
fucking, the metal bars charred underneath their figures.
Gas leak, crow bar, or first a poisoning
by the sea: in a white house above the dunes
you are set on fire, and fall
into a soap opera of light
pinning you to wood. First cinnamon, then paraffin:
how the incense scent inside a linen rose
stitched to a hat becomes votive
candle wax—the jet fringe band that pressed
tangles to your forehead where your mother would tap
her fingers. But that is from a painting
one-hundred fifty years old. In a church,
the mahogany doors carved with symbols
keep you in the antechamber:
first the scent of your mother's hands, then a room
cold in the morning. I was late for yoga,
my concrete-grey stretch pants tucked into my boots.
She appeared, I thought, in makeup, blue under the eyes,
as though rouge were pushed up her cheeks,
as though her pillow rubbed it there.

An angel's share of whiskey is taken from a barrel by the air.
Talk about how I guessed it would be light enough to walk alone.
How she wore shorts and a hooded sweatshirt. McDonald's
    displayed leaves
& hearts with names on them all over the glass doors
across the street as though you could pass through them into
    autumn,
& through autumn, and be full. The white man
balancing his feet on nothing appeared in the walk sign,
and it was as though I could also decide there was nothing
left in her but the hunger
for another body. It was zombie season. I ate her mind
& left her body: punched face,
eyes opening in greened rims, her throat
ringed with marks I thought she could wash off.

62

N° 44
H. L. HIX

"Is this the time when we compare notes?"

—Nadine Gordimer, *None to Accompany Me*

Others may be called back through its stubborn
wooden door into the cramped café
at the stoop-end of a steep street in old town.
Odd angles. Light left over from yesterday
not suffusing the place, just peering in,
urchin-thin, through steam-fringed panes. Tiny
tabletops. Delicate, china-bright notes: spoon
stirring tea, then set to saucer gingerly.

Not me. I'm returned to dirt and basketball
on my hands, smoke sullen in my jacket,
walking home along the pitted gravel road
from Todd Layt's father's farm. Lines of cattle
ambling barnward. Back behind me, Mr. Layt,
lit, burning trash in a barrel in their yard.

N° 45
BRUCE SNIDER

Why My Father Smells Like the Night

Because he lifted the rusted
cutting shears in the name of his
dead brother and the tree limbs
refused to give. Because
he wore Brut, bear scat
and barley, the idle threats
of birds. Because he wore
barn knot and broken, making
anger look easy. His cologne
filled the house with its cheap
drugstore worry. Whiff
of bacon. Whiff of spade-
split turnip. When his brother
died, he cried for days. Because
the world clung to him, spit
sticky and grease fire. Because
he walked out wearing
manly and make-do. Because
his brother once took him fishing
in Ohio. Because when he went
to the graveyard, the pine trees
released their dark scents. Because
what else would grief
smell like if not black
shadows in the cornfield, if not
the moon's slow bone caught
in the bullfrog's throat?

N° 46
TARFIA FAIZULLAH

Diary

Mother would come into my room
smelling of gardenias to thumb

through the pages tucked below
my sleep-winged pillow.

Some days, when helplessness
is a humidity that balms

the windows of the room
you and I make love, I listen

again to the creased crackle
of that paper I purpled

with the roll call of my wants
and sorrows. You suckle

from my throat the petals
of her perfume's glass bottle

I drank from to slake
my anger's thirst. I call to her

with a mouthful of pollen.
Watch her turn to me.

There are questions we will
never answer. My shadow

blooms behind hers, across
you. We dance like that,

her hand around my throat,
my hand around yours.

I tell you, I was laughing when
the bruises began to blossom.

You kiss the broken stem.
Everywhere, *prem*, steam,

The musk of white flowers.

N° 47
LAURA KASISCHKE

The Country of It

Has no houses, no human beings
Just light to live beneath
No joists no beams
The stillness of windmills
Against no landscape
No breeze
The library with only its
Few loose words, like
Where am I please
And this and now and yet
While a mother sings, Oh little sweet
Oh little sweet
You're above the sky and below the sea

"You've come too early," He
Says, who might be Jesus
Or some other doorman, gatekeeper, horrified
Onlooker, someone
Watching this in her bare feet
In a bedroom
On TV

Or some mistake?
Some simplicity?
Some shiny old-fashioned machine
Or intimacy
As our children awaken
From our shame—
I mean, Our dream

"You've come too late, sweet
Little sweet, we've—" He—

But there is no hour
In this country
And certainly no we
He may try to close the door

(Of course
Who wouldn't try?
To close it on this thing, not even—)

But to unhear again their cries?
To fail them
Once more
Completely?

Completely?
Like prayer?
Like perfume
In the funeral home?
Like poetry?

N° 48
KIKI PETROSINO

Persephone

Tip of the tongue, tip of the knife.

Tip of your rib cage, tipped from view.

Bright tips of lemon trees against train windows.

Tip of the county line, receding.

On the train you drink. *Limonata* in tiny cups.

Brightness on your lips as the train descends.

But love tips your mouth up like a seed.

Forget Mother, traipsing through dead corn.

Mother tipping the old wash-stone to peer beneath.

No one comes with her lungs full of dead leaves.

Pull on your dress. Tip your hands into their gloves.

Each long day pulls from the one before.

Mother's call: dumb plug of clear wax.

Your little ears tip back, like a cat's.

N° 49
STACEY LYNN BROWN

Ramble on Rose/Not Fade Away

for Ruth Plaster

Deadhead meant something different to my gardening
aunt than it did to me, the oily scent of patchouli
greasing unwashed bodies no substitute for soap.
In camper-pocked parking lots, gaunt men in hemp
belts cooked grilled cheese sandwiches on red
eyed burners, bartered shrooms for weed,
called out for a miracle. It was the circus
come to town every spring, and I was always thick
in the middle of it, saucered, the pockets
of my army pants riddled with seeds I'd later try

to plant, but lacking her green thumb, would always
come back empty handed from the fields. She
fed wild raccoons tame, grew koi, fertilized
and mulched for the magnificent
roses that unfolded like offerings, open
fisted, a nautilus unfurled. She'd tamp
down a pack of cigarettes, flick
her plastic light, and set about her garden
while I communed with the unwashed
and the holy. I never told time by show dates,

never grieved Pigpen, only the spectacle
of it all, the darkened arena aloft
in a haze of smoke, malnourished
girls in long silk skirts whirling
like seedlings in the backlit portals
between sections, arms
stretched out as if to catch
the very air and rise,
the muted harmonics of Jerry's
guitar pinioning paint, open mouthed

wahwah a trickling treacle, half-stepping down.
On hawked t-shirts, Calvin and Hobbes swung it
on Shakedown Street, skulls blossomed fragrant
into red, and always the stratospheric whorl
of tie-dyes, free fodder for the trip. Those nights
I crashed at her house, too stoned
to go home, she'd wait up
for me to come down, the incessant
thrumming of drum circles lingering
in my head for days. She'd smoke. We'd

smoke. Years later, as she breathed
beneath the oxygen mask that tethered her
to this world like an astronaut
on a walk from the capsule, I still
wouldn't quit. It was something
I carried with me like those
mercurial melodies, the tracer notes
that still come unbidden. *Have a good
show*, Deadheads would say to each other
as hello and goodbye. Hello. Goodbye.

Somewhere, I still have a pack
of her cigarettes, snaked from her bedside
table after she died, *Virginia Slims* still
shrink wrapped, unbreathed. Somewhere,
the ticket stubs and sweat stained set lists, the songs
that bled one into another like colors down a face,
each segue a signpost to make sure you journeyed back:
Help/Slip
Scarlet/Fire
The Music Never Stopped

N°50
LINDSAY LUSBY

Elegy with Osage-Orange

This mockery smashed open
is surely not grief (for as much
as any citrus can be). But maybe

it's love? This inedible mess
of bitter milk and seeds
moldering in the yard

is nothing like you thought it
would look. Or, God forbid,
you give it a taste. But maybe

that dimmed breath of orange
you catch when your eyes close
really is forgiveness

for withdrawing into your
green wrinkled heart when she was
waiting in the house to die.

N° 51
CARRIE JERRELL

Little Elegy for a Childhood Friend

Mostly
incomprehensible,
this pain that follows
your death—a raven

in my chest, a scrim
laid over the brain,
the whole world
clotted with it—

except for the brief
mercy of this evening,
when, of all
the perfume's notes,

its amber
and ginger and rose,
what lifts highest from
my warm wrist

is the bitter orange
you would have loved,
the means of the scent's
journey

so much like your
body's departure,
through heat,
through smoke,

to pass from one form
into another
and into another
I cannot see—

then,
as the star hour
blooms and birds
still themselves in the trees,

I believe it,
that you are among
all of these small beauties,
and know them again.

N° 52
PATRICK PHILLIPS

Green Irish Tweed

You can hear someone laughing. It's only
your brother, and one of his pot-smoking friends.
You twist the gold cap of your father's cologne.

It's late: the Lake House. The grown-ups all gone.
You touch the chrome razor and wince.
Outside someone laughs, but it's only

your brother, yelling *totally, totally stoned.*
Were you ever that flickering flame of a kid,
cheeks cold with your father's cologne?

Remember that house? By the lake, in the woods.
The grown-ups were coming home when?
Your brother starts crying. You're ten, only

ten. In the mirror, you're still forty-one,
wearing a face that your father wore then.
Every Christmas, that flask of cologne.

Your brother still lovely, your father still strong.
Everything still so far ahead
you hear someone say. But it's you, only

you, at the mirror alone.
Your brother outside with his friends.
What was the name on that flask of cologne?

Someone unknowingly sent you some once,
like a door to that house in the past,
where you stand at a mirror, in the woods, all alone.
Where you breathe, and your father comes home.

N°53
DAN BELLM

Fur

I am still young enough to be allowed to stand to the side and watch him transform, leaning at the bathroom mirror in his white undershirt and shorts to shave with the electric razor after showering away his roughness or most of it, the grease and the sweat. He is not a hairy man, but there is the fur of his forearms and his legs. Unapproachable in his concentration. Has never once pressed me to his chest. They are going out tonight, Mom in the fox stole that was his gift, soothing to pet with the back of a hand and lined with pale pink satin: the way a man shows love. Have I tried to wear it? I know already this is not quite right. How could you wear a thing like that, the head still attached, and not think of it biting your neck? A sharp sweetness in the musk of his aftershave all through the room that makes me want to drink it. Later I will: a sip, a swig: wishing to be so rare a creature, naked but for the rough coat of scented black hairs on my face: then the dark reverse of its amber and alcohol when I have to puke it up. He is the only animal allowed in the house. Then comes the white shirt and tie, the creased black pants. He is complete: he turns away and is out the door, leaving a fog of musk and hair, leaving his shadow to settle on my skin. But I am not the shadow; I am not anyone yet; I will shed this body for another.

N° 54
JAMES ALLEN HALL

Not Her Body

Her mouth jarred open by breathing duct,
chest rhythmic under the starched sheet.
A skin scoured clean as a polished floor
in an emptied house, for sale. Gone, the garden
grit underneath her fingernails, she was never
less her hands. Not her body, I thought.
The heart took forty minutes without breath
to stop. At the funeral, not a flower
in sight, I caught the dark purple smell
of her ungloved hands, crossing over to me,
and I could see her pruning the plum tree,
gritting her teeth, planting the geranium
out back. But she was dead, and we were
at the cemetery, burying my grandmother alive.

N°55
SARAH ARVIO

Eau de cologne (hardly a flower)

Oh the cologne

of my granddad
bright hard dry   no fruit

hardly a flower
oh colonist of a faint fizz

with a colonial air
upright old colonist

a pat on the shaven cheek
few words   no fruit

hardly a flower
fought in the first war

but never said where
and was wounded

but never said where
could it be Cologne?

a flower in his buttonhole
a handkerchief in his hand

he was all buttoned down
and all buttoned up

lived a long life
died of cancer of the colon

drinking eau de cologne
too many dour thoughts

few words   no fruit
hardly a flower

N° 56
ERIKA MEITNER

L'Etrog

At first, the bottom of my
grandmother's European purse
with the thick gold clasp, then

the citrusy musk wears thin
on my pulse points and I am New York
in its almost dusk, after work, nearly-

summer glory; I am spike heels
on pavement, I am air the temperature
of skin when happy hour spills over

from storefronts toward the river.
I am not the crying baby, I am
no longer the hinterlands.

For a moment I forget
about plastic and Walmart,
interstate and diapers and become

the rouged past, hazy, glorified—
someone's Upper East Side date
washed in lemon and money.

I have borrowed Mariya's
Astor Place sublet for the week—
she pressed the key into my hand

along with two white ecstasy tablets
wrapped in tinfoil before she left again
for South America, so I bring you

back there and we are alone
in this city with the air-conditioning
huffing, with the tall windows

sealed shut in someone else's
sheets: we are June and so high
above the possibility that fills

the avenues with neon
buses and weaving taxis
and lights flickering on

since it is dark now—it is dark
and I am resting my palm
on the skin of your back

while all the people swim
downtown toward us like salmon.
This is not Mediterranean night—

it is Manhattan; it is home
but we whisper to each other
in Hebrew and then it's Jerusalem

and we're on a roof somewhere
on Har Hatzofim with the stones
and olive trees. I look at pictures

and it all comes back: it is always
dark and I am holding your hand
in the street since there are things

to do here after sunset—I am holding
your thrumming hand at the end
of the dock and the water tells me

I am a groupie, a junkie,
a department store hussy
but this scent argues back:

I am figs and honey, balm and bounty,
sweet cabin of palm leaves, beautiful
lemon trees held steady with one hand:

you twist off the fruit cradled
like an arm in a sling or bees
in a hive—a careful living object

wrapped in silk, tucked
in a silver box: and you shall take,
and you shall rejoice.

N° 57
LESLIE HARRISON

[Render]

Render the honey this late plunder vexed infected

theft this twice stolen sweetness render sweetgrass

smoke and flower rive this bud this first unfolding

first lacey pale purchase of the never to be born this

first fisted cling render rain spatter and pock this

skycold falling render pollen ticking in the throat in

the lungs render this pluck and petalsnow adrift this

smudge of scent in the air render memory as this as

dream as foretelling as Cassandra mouth taped hands

tied to keep her terrible swirling her galaxies her stars

born in dust and fire to keep them safe and away

render her flutter her vivid come hither of nectar

and sun-warmed fruit her whisper of the nearly born

and newly freshly dead rent torn and boiled down

render unto Cassandra that which is stolen that which

is infant sweet and sweet nearly to rot render unto us

this cold season this wish as yet unfulfilled render

unto winter this clear glass prison misprision this

treason to time and every gorgeous delicate thing

this downed captured gathered spring this nest of

sand and fire this small vial this tiny perfect violence

N° 58
MELODY S. GEE

Gravid

You swim in me to feed and breathe.
The gulps of fluid in your lungs are
your lungs. Into them, what has already
traveled me. If I breathe
a stamen, you are stamen.
If I taste bitter salt, you are char
and ash. What do you take
when I take in another's body?
What when I soak my neck in this oil that sings
gardenia but is not flower?

The journey inside me has
something to do with blood,
carrying on it like barges the wide outside
you already taste, and all you will soon see.
I suck this sodden spring air down to you
and everything is dying.
Everything is beginning to loosen, drop
its seeds, and say
what's needed is done.

They come up from the ground, these shoots.
They come out of the trees, these flowers to fruit,
and the air parts for them,
the fired dirt swaddles the ready germ.
There is so much ahead now, there is only
time to unravel and disclose.

Your cells are dividing to build you
and yet, like the rest of us,
you begin dying too.
We take our time, and while we gorge on for more,
what we have eaten is eaten forever.

N° 59
ERIN BELIEU

Victoria Station

When a girl is the disaster,

mostly minor, the thing gone
wonky before even attempted,
too sticky to clean;

the obvious, unsolvable,
an appliance with directions
lost in the junk drawer. When

a wreck, red-haired,
red-faced, this clown of a girl,
unfunny, is urgent as the red

lacquered phone box
she bawls into weekly, fears
herself the character

whose paragraphs you skip—

then the tea shop
near Victoria Station,
cologne of pears wicking from

the door. Then the fleur-de-lis
of freesia bunched at every
table where ladies idle in

sturdy skirts. A shelter,

all quiet, a shop with an owner
who sets a girl down, weightless,
a cup, transparently boned.

Who never knows kindness
will be a map: the scent of pears
and freesia, white stones

on a path, the driftwood
she clings to when disguised as
a beggar, this girl asleep

on the hero's beach.

N° 60
JEANNINE HALL GAILEY

Safran Troublant

It's troubling: the stain from the stamen
of crocus flowers, the way vanilla scraped from the pod,
sticky and damp, clings to fingers.

You can smell the heat and syrup of plants
blooming at night. The passionflower you sip
at bedtime. It's the trouble you bring

into the room of nicotine and oldest bourbon, worn leather,
with your walk, with your easy stance,
the growl and sweetness of your ready mouth.

N° 61
ELISA GABBERT

Consider the Rose

A woman's point of view is the third person:
She smells her own perfume. A rose

just is feminine—it's built into the language.
Consider the mean rose, the frigid rose

dipped in liquid nitrogen and shattered
on the tabletop. Pink inside red.

Or the lush rose dying, slumped
with the weight of its beauty. But always

the icy edge, at the top of the back
of the throat, shrill when it speaks

of a memory. Regret is the future
of hope. In every woman, a girl,

and in the girl, the long desire,
the waiting to be ravaged.

N° 62
JULIANA GRAY

Vanille Abricot Comptoir Sud Pacifique

I've never been sweet, but two dabs
behind the ear, and I'm a sugar cookie,
a walking confection, light as vanilla meringue.

I walked downtown, past a park where children
abandoned slides, tumbled like chimpanzees
from the jungle gym, begging their mothers for candy.

The ice cream parlors were mobbed for tutti-frutti.
The bakeries sold out of snickerdoodles,
shortbread, ladyfingers, then barred their doors.

I had a craving, too, so stepped inside
a hipster bar. The patrons' nostrils flared;
they tossed their PBRs and ordered rounds

of craft cocktails with muddled apricot,
agave nectar, blood oranges,
vermouth and local cider. Their jaws ached

for a taste of me. One skinny boy
followed my trail, through the town gone mad
for sweetness, back to my cottage in the woods.

He told me his name as I peeled away his jeans,
but I just called him Hansel. The skinny boys
are all called Hansel, and they fatten up just fine.

N°63
ERICA DAWSON

Chronic

I know the moon's persistent but a dead
Woman is rigor, more moonlight and branch
Than moonlight on a branch. I want to cut
My teeth on her. Her skin holds dawn's illusion.
Postmortem piss dries yellow on her thigh.

I don't know why she dies or who she is,
Whether I murder her in quiet sleep
Because I can't dream dying, or because
I'm literary and need metaphors.

I do know moons are just a phase away
From their returns, and she is always there.
I've missed her more than enough to touch her in
What once was dew; hear her in rain that spits
Just like an ever-circling scavenger.

Night wears her now on its forehead in spots
Only a mother smells. There, in her rigor,
She smells of thunderstorms distilled in mulch,
Perfumed with petals closing moon-white plumes
To suckle honey—star anise, lime zest.

I sense her freesia in a zephyr's crook.

But I envy her night-blue artery
Looking hawkish enough to crack like hoarfrost.

N° 64
MARI L'ESPERANCE

End of Empire

Such abundance wasn't meant to last—

       the fairy queen harbored in her hive

of silks, ripe extravagance of blackberry

       and bergamot, night jasmine and mandarin

an intoxicating swoon—such luxuriance

       was doomed from the start. Unseen beneath

her honeyed cell, hung with heavy velvet

       and brocade, spread the stain of stolen

mahogany and ruin—a dream of plum,

       persimmon, lush tumble of peonies

and wisteria quietly bruising at its heart.

       Alone in her scented bower, the last candle darkened,

she thought she could hear the whispers of fate

       among the exhalations of fainting blossoms.

N° 65
MATHIAS SVALINA

Nicolle Writes Those Girls With The
or, Tobacco Vanille from Tom Ford

Nicolle writes *those girls with the BO that smells like cumin and its so intoxicating and sex i am so jealous of them. i just dont have the estrogen.* I write back *I always wished I smelled like freshly ground black pepper. I told this to my friend Joanna who writes romance novels & she said that was a common trope in romance novels for describing men: peppery. I want to be peppery.* A woman I went on a sad date with told me that I didn't smell as dirty as she thought I would. It wasn't sad during the date. It was sad in the days after the date. Rachel loved a room that smelled like sweaty men. She'd get a look in her eyes. She talked about pheromones like they are magic. The woman I kissed in Vermont while I was engaged to Rachel wore an unwashed fleece pullover she'd sprayed with perfume that smelled like money. The combination of the perfume & her made me want to set myself on fire & so I set myself on fire. When I'm not home my dog pulls my shirts from the laundry basket & makes a nest of them on the couch & lies on it. When I get home I ask him *Did you make a nest? Are you the best nestmaker? Are you?* Courtney, at a !!! show in Manhattan during the trip when she stopped loving me, said that, though he was eighty feet away & hundreds of sweating, dancing people surrounded us, she could smell the singer & I believed her. Julia said good genetic mates can smell this in each other. A friend of hers once texted her that he'd walked into an empty hall in an empty building & the hall smelled like her. In high school I had a Holy Rollers t-shirt & Erik wanted to borrow it but I told him it was dirty but he said he didn't care. The next day he told me the shirt hadn't smelled bad & he put it on but then he smelled the pits & they smelled horrible & the way he said the word horrible made his eyes look like this: *~~* *~~*. Though Julia moved out more than a year ago boxes of her things are still in my apartment & sometimes I'll come home to find one of her gloves or t-shirts in my dog's nest & I'll know he opened a box in the closet that was closed just to get to the smell of her.

N° 66
CAKI WILKINSON

Redolent

She wore Rose Water & Vanilla.
She wore an era's vow, all rite,
all anther & sorrow. A wise Eve,
a variant, she wore eros well
or was ethereal in love's war.
She wore rose a la wilt, raven
& real ravish; wore stolen awe,
seawater, ravines, & hollower
weather; wore roses & vanilla,
& her answer was to roil—leave
a slow verse, a trail nowhere.

N° 67
YONA HARVEY

"I was seduced by the independence of his mind"

—interview with Jean-Paul Millet Lage of
Maître Parfumeur et Gantier, *Ça Fleure Bon*

You never wear cologne. You give
& you give & you give & you give.
& they take.You
are mine. Or so you say,
winking. I want to tell that stupid girl
to shut the hell up about the sonnet.
You shrug. Just a girl, you say.
You once saw seabirds in her
skirt—a blue, irregular outline,
a neglected island. & anyway,
cologne is for boys. Just don't tell
the young lovers too soon. Give them
the feathered headdresses & coconuts
they imagine, the little trees that bear chocolate fruit.

N° 68
DEBORAH LANDAU

Roseberry

I was paddling around the lake in my wedding dress
wondering who deposited me
in this quiet white.

A taxi would save time.
A tattoo would liven me up.
A grand idea, that's what someone said.

Tidy vial, *roseberry*,
in which they invented monogamy
and taught the girls what to long for,

petticoats rubbing shoulders
with motorcycle jackets
and moonboots,

memories and lust, protestations of love
the grip of commitment, walls erupting
in blooms, unruly, vine-covered, thick

with birds' nests, liquid seeping
from the treetops, ceiling.
Well, what did you expect?

It's a man-made lake, a mirror.
And something violet rioting around it.
Wild raspberries, threatening stain.

If I drink too much,
if I lose my inhibitions,
will I get them back?

N° 69
MICHELLE CHAN BROWN

Fable

In every woman's private film, a Mata Hari dances
to the freewheel rune of *oui*.
The devil's cameo is bland.

In every woman's diary, the only month is May.
She rings the buzzers of the beautiful
until her fingers blue.
She locks god out of her mother's
house, calls it a museum.
She bleeds her father's mistresses,
calls it perfume.

In every woman's life, no one comments
on the blood-dredged hem,
the hierarchy: animal trumps heroine.
So childhood ends—the ribbons
hug a box with nothing in it.
The skies, occasionally kind.
The season, spent.

The convent burns,
each nun convinced in what she's owed.
And marriage merely acquisition:
prettier empty bowls.
The hands bathing the mothers
are dark with oil.
The mothers, old and suddenly.
Their tendons itch with summer.
The fathers, alone in the kitchen,
licks butter from the knives.

A woman grown is outcast
by the forest creatures, dumb
as she is to her own scent.
She eats peach after peach
to sweeten her sweat.
Weeds whiten above her bed.

Prides of the village, go on
and French kiss all the wrongs
until they cry.
If she can bottle this,
surely someone will pay.

N° 70
MARY BIDDINGER

The Most & the Best

My heart was just a series of dashes.
Nobody else was available to star

in this particular flip-book. Imagine
a burned out wooden bathhouse.

It's true that all roads have scabs.
Volcanic soap and children in terry

halters. So many of us packed
into a tattered blue Thunderbird.

Inflation of hair on Woodward
Avenue. We gazed at the street like

a beach gazes back at mismatched
lovers. Sea-clang, walls of weed.

I never wanted to be anyone's
animal. A woman packed unripe

fruit into a busted speaker, let
the electricity fly. I buried my face

in a stack of last winter's best
misgivings, white cotton tablecloths

left helpless above all the jasmine.
I resembled an adolescent

melon half buried in a yard.
My dermatologist once theorized

that I resembled Audrey Hepburn
in her *jeunesse*. Perhaps this

was just meant to be ironic. My hair
freshly washed with bucket water.

N° 71
DAWN LONSINGER

Antoinette

Out of the bus and into the afternoon we
descended, smelling of rubber cement and vinyl.
That's her—gone giddy in the negligent sun.

Antoinette flipping her hair like an ocean wave
so it fell again and again, a dark hem across her back.
Antoinette tooting her recorder between houses halted

in foundations. Antoinette of adult words: of *fuck*,
and *damn*, and *blow job*. Antoinette of basement gin.
Antoinette of Thorndale, PA, of Couldn't Care Less.

Truth is the woods were full of ticks but you said *let's
cut through*, said *you have lots of blood, plenty to share*.
We spat into the heads of dandelions to make cocktails

while the lilacs by the edge of the road leaked tart sugar
to tempt bees into the evermore deranged air. We weren't
about to *head straight home*, sutured instead the gash

of asphalt with our curious back-and-forth bodies,
our honeysuckle promiscuity. Antoinette of stain
and loll, of not missing a thing and not knuckling under.

Once you lifted your shirt and showed me your nipples
which, unlike mine, had begun to swell away from you.
They looked like the softest buttons, halved olives.

Antoinette of inauguration and Now & Laters,
you smelled like forever, which is—I understand—wildness
cored by knowledge. If it weren't for the hazard of your eyes

upon me, I might have buried my face in a bank
of lilac bushes, might have never come back to the world
in time to see the sun blotted out by clouds, a storm ripping

the sky in half like a failed draft, in time to see
our parents divorced, furniture shimmied into U-Hauls,
Andy losing his eye to a rogue lawn mower blade.

Do you remember, Antoinette, the time we lay down
in Mrs. Ackers' garden, the carrots we were not allowed
to eat dirt-dark beneath our backs, all our envy grounded?

Because of you, my Antoinette, I knew that if I entered
the fray at dusk I'd be an element of weather, a clattering, a clot,
lightning bugs constellating my mind, the smell of lazy boys

and Spam so far away they would never reach me. Elsewhere,
of course, there are other Antoinettes who jump rope, who lick
the edges of cheap ice cream sandwiches, who have a thing

or two to say about cake.

N° 72
JESSICA PIAZZA

Too pretty for words

A cloying offering: this summer's heat, the cheerful greenery deadheaded blooms leave, a leering gaze, a heart's alarming beat when greeted by her nearness. *(So soon, she'll come to fear this.)* All her woes are overthrown by dusk; its orange light, its perching on the cusp of something lovely. Breathing the musk and lily breeze eases her, belief seizing her: sweet air can only mean a sweeter meeting. Until that evening. Slowly graying amber light. A lamp left lit for when he comes. But none of what he says is good. And none of the cautions she'd been warned of dulled his maddening, clanging anger. *(Nothing, none. He just gets himself gone.)* Deep into night, she laments what's lost. She runs to the river, she falls to the moss. The rough black tree's bark bears her up; she tentatively steps, collecting blossoms as she tiptoes branch to branch, a nymph, a laugh that madly ricochets. Mourning what's alive and what decays. Beneath her, fallen flowers, bright and fragrant, rot in the water. They woo their fragile daughter down to the depths below. She gasps; she only grasps at rue. She does not rise. No rose, no jasmine coaxes her back home. *(She dies alone.)*

N° 73
MOIRA EGAN

Mon Parfum Chéri, Par Camille

She glides into the room. Her velvet skirts
drag, languid, hem come half undone, a wake
(*there's many a one shall find out all heartache*)
of violet and iris, queer tinctures.

The candles flicker. Lavender shadows
cavort in corners, porphyry to plum.
Our host sees her, greets her with a salaam,
(and *finding that her voice is sweet and low*)

and kisses her, guides her to the window.
He deftly lights her Gauloises, strokes her palm,
her skin not young, but smoothed with years of balm
(because *"to be born woman is to know—"*)

She rustles in her bag, pulls out a bottle,
that purple wine whose grape is named for tears,
a stone-walled garden, overgrown for years
(and *we must labour to be beautiful.*)

N° 74
JERICHO BROWN

American Masculinity

Because I am silent

You want to hear

From me. Because

I have color, you will

Taste me. Bergamot

And grapefruit, pimento

And Jamaica pepper,

Elemi and saffron,

Leather and tobacco.

Say cocktail of virility.

Say implosion before

I explode. My spice

Prominent when you

Pull the pin where spiky

Pepper and cinnamon

Intertwine before I take

A short detour down

The amber way. Say

Vanilla and I slap you,

Strike you like a good-
Looking grenade.

N° 75
JOHN POCH

Please

The difference between a glass
of sunlight and your throat
in water is not so simple. Hollows.

Keep your hair up all day
so I can pretend I'm at the ocean.

If you could unroll
the fingers of my hand
from its fist of hardship,
you would see a map of lines,
or a tough palm and tougher prints
destined for turning Bible paper
late night by lamplight.
You might sense cinnamon.
Sugar in the cut wood of juniper.

Like a child enamored
with a tangerine,
I lose myself
peeling the rind away
in one slow whole,
forgetting the present.

This is a fault, and this is
how I love your clothes.

N° 76
SANDY LONGHORN

Too Simple a Reason

The other woman wore perfume
peppered with citrus peel and zest,
hot, tropical exotics embedded

at her wrists, her neck, a flagrant
dab between her flaunted breasts.

Behind a secretary desk, she lay in wait
on barren winter days, painted her lips
when she heard your truck arrive

so you would catch her in the act,
that lipstick angled, poised,

sensual and slick. You'd only just
kissed Mother on a bare cheek,
her skin rinsed with the scent

of Dial soap, her hands plunged
in greasy dishwater gone cold.

You'd only just hollered goodbye
as we three stuffed our backpacks
with homework and a stash

of dime-store makeup we'd apply
at school, the fluorescent bathroom

lights a garish tool. Perfume the one
luxury we forbade ourselves, unable
to scrub our bodies clean of the smell

before the last bell and the bus ride
home across gravel roads windblown

to icy dangers. All winter secrets gathered
just beneath our skin, cheeks and lips
chapped raw by a frigid, unscented wind.

N° 77
DAVID MASON

My Mediterranean

The smell of her skin
at the collar, her laughter
a fluent belonging—

oranges of winter,
grass after rain,
sweet-bitter where
my tongue wants to crawl.

I hymn the sea
between winter and spring,
everything she
has turned into song,

breathe in the smoke
of sawed olive limbs
after the harvest,
leather and amber.

What is an earth
but a dark sweet smell?
What is love
but a lucent pool

for diving in?
The smell of her skin,
her hair in the sun,

come to me now
my moment of want.
All flesh is dew,

all earth is breath
and she is the sea
between word and word.

The smell on our skin,
mine not hers,
hers not mine,

Mediterranean.

N°78
MARK BIBBINS

Dear Rotten Garden—

—who could bear to live next
to your wet humping sound—

—well I realize people do
absurd things in the world

they take off their skin
and don't touch me—

—from a height I am some sweet

girl   albeit one who squeezed
when she meant to swerve—

—having amassed a weddingful
of nuisances and sword-tasting—

—having moved prudently and shoeless

away   I could hear   you behind me

spitting perverted economies—

—also having been the painter
who takes your instructions

among them nothing
about painting

but what translates to *roll around on me*

like you're putting out a fire—

Nº 79
BETH BACHMANN

unspeakable

Two things that cannot be must be

first stone, then star. Mother of all monsters, father of all
monsters, why

did you make me thus: tireless fox? Dog that eats whatever it
wants,

unbeatable beast, at least we have the sky nightly, a view

of the whole battle. God cannot survive here.

He demands to be named. Unknown soldier, you hardly say you
love me but you love me like the ice

the orchid takes slowly in its turning toward light.

In a garden, every bloom is somatic. I thought you wanted fire.

You want peace. You're facing a wall.

I am a species only you can claim.

N° 80
CARMEN GIMÉNEZ SMITH

That One Night

Is my favorite place with its curved topographies,
as if a rose petal also canyon. I tease the scent-notes from
your nameless transgressions like in the stories little girls love
    because
they last for days and contain ravishments. Undoing your climate
makes bodies some smells, like the spider that comes at me
when I'm just a telescope in the copse. Her silk is spire-hot
with ardor and her hex palaver calls a trap down onto me, a fur
    net.
You're a dozen stars ringed and avowed, the old ones up, the
    others
falling and pouring wet tears for ceremony, a blowout you call it.
Had we been strangers, we might haven't.

N° 81
BRIAN BARKER

Dream in Which We Eat the World

for Nicky

Creamed calf's brain and vodka
        in a farmhouse outside Kraków.
Blood sausage and cold tripe salad.

Borscht that sends a flush
        down your neck and collarbone.
Our hostess, a crone who recites Mickiewicz,

her enormous breasts shaking
        as she cackles and fans you
with her apron. Her scent comes

in black waves, licorice and berry blintzes,
        and we swoon on the hot winds
of Santiago, where we eat smoked

pig's cheek smothered in fire ant jam,
        rolled in plantain leaves,
served in a box like expensive cigars. . . .

The peasants drag the dead dictator
        from the palace.
They dump him in a field of thistles

as bees buzz the soft skin behind his ears
        where he dabbed cologne
each morning, cedar and orange peel

lifting on the breeze, and we're drowsing
        off again, now a pair of spotted goats
in love, nibbling his gold epaulets,

eating the cuffs off his silk shirt. . . .
        But still we scarf down goat
heart tartare in Barcelona,

bone marrow on brown bread,
        giblets with a little salad
of violet blossoms dressed in squid's ink

that you lick from the plate.
        In San Miguel de Allende, our tongues
savor tongue tacos with pickled onions

bought from a child riding a blind burro.
        We eat them in silence
in one bite, then drink cold beer

under a jacaranda tree, toasting love
        and good luck, confessing
our appetites, Southern and Jewish,

which conjure the next meal
        before the last has even settled.
In Venice, octopus carpaccio

with a dollop of urchin roe,
        drizzled with olive oil,
sliding on a plate as big as a hubcap

as the room tilts and green seawater
        rushes beneath the door,
sloshing with claw and kelp, sardines

shimmering in the candlelight.
        Our waiter brings more wine,
galoshes, cracks his towel at an eel

clinging to the tablecloth,
        then sweeps his hand down
over the teeming dark waters:

Tonight, for you lovers, any desire you want.

N° 82
ALISON STINE

Rose Ikebana

When I try to trace this story I cannot find it.
I cannot remember: Don Juan or Casanova,
someone, someone drove a woman so mad

with love, when he asked her to sit on a chair,
she did, for weeks never rising, never
turning, waiting for him, shaking, starved—

Outside the hotel, snow slid off the roof
and smacked against the pavement. Winter
disappeared. A seagull wheeled.

The doorman's whistle for a cab ricocheted
off curbs and bricks and carried. You woke,
tangled in my scent. I thought I had never felt

more alive. I made the mistake of telling you.
The sky was blue as glass, blood still flecking
my body, curved to the cup of your hand.

I should have said: *Salt, write your name
inside my belly.* I should have said: *Mark me,
claim me, bind me to the bone.* He asked her

to sit on a chair and turn away from him,
so she did not see him leave, only heard
the murmur of the door, felt the shudder,

the pressure of him not returning
and not returning and not returning and not—
I have felt that wafting off us for years.

I have wanted to apologize. I have wanted
to beg. I have always, always been opening
for you with every silence, every absence,

every year with the softest of cries. Know:
This time, when you entered me, I did not
remove my heart for you, but rather, shifted it

to the side—where I wait, on a chair.

N° 83
BRYNN SAITO

The Farmer

Still he goes on. Seeking her scent. Ghost of him grown
past a century. She's old too, her spirit quick with match-wit
and subtle charm. It's night in the summer valley. So I imagine
    them
young again: touching under peach trees, moon streaming
through the matrix, orchards alive with God knows what.
Quick taste of tenderness before the empire of addiction,
quick glimpse of a life drenched in moonlight instead of fire.
Her father brought his gun out and faced her in the front yard
but she married my grandfather anyway. Story goes his beauty
was the talk of the town. Now she turns again toward him
like she did as a girl, turning toward his shoulders, his perfumes
of dust. What can we do but release her? *You are supple
like sandalwood*, I sing to myself. *When she slips through flame
in the final hour may you follow then return as smoke.*

N° 84
LISA D. CHÁVEZ

Afternoon Ghosts

Scent of sea and oranges: a day decades past
rushes back. Sultry afternoon, French spoken
with the island lilt. Was he a poet? A painter?

You don't recall, but you see that fine, clever
face. Skin dark against a linen shirt, and in his hand
the fruit: flesh gem red, the scent's bright burst.

Not a pomegranate, and you no Persephone, still
the act seeded with what couldn't be. His somber smile
as if he saw it all: the lines you wouldn't cross,

the country's collapse. A last kiss, the way you'd leave
looking back. Your hands shook. Demitasse cups
and coffee bitter black. So much restraint.

For what? The proper husband, the narrow path
you took? Gone now, and you beached
on this balcony, marooned in memory. And regret.

For all that was offered, all you didn't take:
a man's hand. Blood oranges on a chipped china plate.

N° 85
ADRIAN MATEJKA

In Algebra Class, Prince Stuck in My Head

The beautiful ones bling like the faux gold
chain greening on the pretty girl's neck
in front of me. Its suspect lineage, its shaky
clasp halved by happenstance like each
of the numerals in an algebraic stem. Green
sweat breaking on her leaf-shaped collars,
sweat on every leaf-strung tree we wished
for in HUD housing. Potholes & chair-boosted
doors where a dinner table should be. Math's
empty sweat in my mother's purse where
an afro pick & some food stamps would be
if mom took the assistance. & the forked stiletto
of equations sulking around the chalkboard—
our local villain, a misunderstood teenager
with a slick cigarette instead of an equal sign.
She should have been in high school by now,
moving south along an infinite series of Jheri
curls. Instead, she's got a driver's license
& plays on the 8th grade basketball team.
Algebra will not get her out of this jam.
No matter how humiliating her chalked visit
to the board. No matter how directly her pencil
makes a falsetto out of my palm. Our first
kiss is an equation of the five most abrupt
numbers I could come up with as we spun past
graffitied underpasses on a purple motorcycle,
eyeliner on the streets instead of median lines,
the skyline's bare knuckles & our eyes as low
as hat brims with lace trim. All of this wrapped
in a sunrise like the early-to-rise geeks who can
make a sentence from any number. All of this,
exactly like the answers in the back of the book.

N° 86
ILYSE KUSNETZ

Blue Amber

Perfume is heat. Perfume
below the ice of sleep. As from one
shore to another, dreams rivulet,

molecules of citrus and musk
floating above our sheets. When you toss
not quite awake, your pillow burns

lily spice, clove and river grass,
civet and cinnamon, poems you wrote
in desert heat, brass and something

earthier, the Grand Bazaar in Istanbul,
hand-knotted carpets of wool and silk—
each knot a moment, every perfume a book.

Remember the story of the lonely murderer
who had no scent—though he possessed
the keenest olfactory sense in Paris.

With oils wrung from a brace of virgins,
he created a scent so sublime
that people, inspired to a frenzy of pure love,

tore him to pieces when he wore it.
His last thoughts were of amber,
the mother who'd abandoned him in a basket of fish.

Last night I dreamed of whales
and Italian poets, woke
to the sweet aftermath of rain on the lilacs.

Page by vanishing page
it enters you like a lover's touch,
so light, you mistake it for your own skin.

N° 87
BRIAN TURNER

Blue Amber (Reprise)

Last night, as I dreamed of whales
singing beneath the moonlit waters of Lake Adair,

you held my hand and spoke of Italian poets, the wake
of our conversation given darkness and the thin clear panes

of tiny wings. Your voice, sweet in the rain and fall
of language, tended to the design of a vast architecture

we discovered circling the lake, each word perfectly
fitted to the vault of the cerebellum. We kissed then, two

lovers under the weight of history, where we, the damaged, touched
one another beneath dead stars and oak trees and Spanish moss,

the distant light of planets a dusting of blue amber on our skin.
I closed my eyes to breathe in the union of notes

rising from the tips of your hair, the night's perfume a
brightening heat
gathered from the minute flames contained within all things.

Over the curvature of the Earth, glaciers calved ice as I slept on.
You walked hand in hand beside me, guiding me

in the construction of the far shore, the landscape of the dream
given fliers on reconnaissance over the waters beyond us

while you continued to house each thing with a name, saying
citrus, musk,
the cry of the great blue heron a recognition of the darkness
receding

as you did so, my body floating in the blue sheets of our bed
as word by word you widened the imagination outward. Love,

I don't want to wake now. I'll rest my head on the pillow
the way sailors once carved wooden spoons with their thoughts
   to stern.

I'll remember the redolent cloves, the deep wet grass, the wheels
   of hay
smoldering in the afternoon light, blackberries sugaring your
   tongue,

cinnamon in the kiss of your lips, and I'll think of the light of
   New York
discovering the vocabulary of desire within us, and how your
   poems

span the amphitheater of the world, reminding me of the heat
   and brass
of our bodies joining together, the deserts and oceans within us,

the wild earth we've wandered to find each other, from Istanbul
to the infinite torii of the vermillion gates at Fushimi Inari.

I once asked for your hand on a bridge of silk over the Lake of
   Love
as twenty-seven swans served as witnesses in a silent assembly
   below.

Each word, love, and every gesture since a continuation of those
   vows.
Each word and every gesture since a lamp in the shadows

of my life, that cliché of unavoidable story, the loneliness of
   years gone by
part of the man whose hand you now hold, part of the distant
   staring I have,

part of the broken nature of who I am, part of the scent you
   recognize,
your presence a reminder that a spatial and temporal world offers
   renewal,

your presence a refutation of the façade of Paris, the hollow
   nature
of romance written of in books and spoken of by characters in
   plays

all I had then, as I sat in empty rooms, lacking oil and flame, wringing
my hands, dreaming of a lover across the water, of you, of a lover

beyond the harsh cries of gulls wheeling over baskets of fish
and the hard voices of men and women deep in their lifelong harvest.

I cannot know if my last thoughts will be of the ambered hues
of dawn filtering through the blinds to brighten your hair

as you sleep beside me. When it comes time for me to wake,
I don't want to leave the world you've lifted into language and light

for us to share, so much more than scent and vision and touch—a sublime
gift, to experience another world transposed within, by leaf and branch

and blade of grass, from the light of statues to the monuments of space,
the generations of people astonished by it all, as I am, my love, standing beside you.

N° 88
CRISTIN O'KEEFE APTOWICZ

New Haarlem Bond No. 9

is the name of the perfume that arrived
in my mailbox in a small glass vial exactly
one month after you kissed me good-bye.

The bottle sat on my desk as snow fell
like discarded wedding ribbon all over
the backyard that was the opposite of Texas.

I shoved it in a drawer the weekend you arrived
like birthday cake, the waitresses of my heart
crowding around our small table to sing.

That night the fire smoldered through sudden rain,
as we dragged the guest room mattress in front of it
and rubbed our match tips together.

Oh, Eau de Wet Firewood Snapping to Flame;
Oh, Eau de Bacon Wriggling in the Pan; Oh,
Eau de Your Soap married to the Eau de Your Skin;

Oh, Jesus, the Eau de Us, trailing me after you left,
our beautiful song, so quiet and bird-throated,
this small ghost appearing out of nowhere.

Weeks later, I twist the black cap of the glass vial
not sure of what to expect: the smell of New York?
Spit on hot asphalt and steam through filthy cement.

All the salted flesh riding on it and through it
and seething wild underneath it? That life I lived,
the smell of me before you?

Oh perfume, you were so simple, so sweet and spice,
leather and musk, light and new. Still, I couldn't,
returning you to your drawer, the pens and tape.

Oh perfume, it wasn't that you weren't lovely,
it's just you weren't what I wanted: you were not
the small perfect heat of my lover's neck.

N° 89
JASON SCHNEIDERMAN

Scent

It has to be intimate, the sort of thing
I can only pick up when we're close.

Not the cloud of the elderly woman
choking you as she gets on the elevator

or the reek of Axe Body Spray from
the young man on the subway with

too much product in his hair, and too
much skin showing under his club-

going tank top. It's not that you have
to be mysterious; all that leaving

something to the imagination stuff.
It's that when I come in, I have to

recognize it as you, the way the scent
has mingled with your chemistry.

Tom Ford said he wanted his cologne
to smell like a man's crotch, which

is a smell it took me forever to adjust to.
I thought it smelled like nuts, ironically,

wondered if that was another origin
of the nickname. Today, I can smell

almost nothing. I open the vial to complete
my assignment, and it brings me back

to Jamey, who I called James, and had
a king-sized bed, and my favorite car

and we broke up in a fight over whether
or not I could name all the members

of the Brat Pack. Before I knew love
or intimacy, I knew sex, and the joy

of a man who knew how to wear cologne,
so perfectly that it came up on you

at just the right time, after I had moved
in close, and my hope of (wretched phrase)

getting lucky had become (gorgeous word)
inevitable.

N°90
SHARA McCALLUM

A Short History of Sex

He'd sit nightly sipping drinks, letting the Coke go flat,
the rum become a watered-down memory.

For weeks she watched him,
until she imagined his life's history

as something to smell and taste, like limes
he twisted into his glass, like sweat

that sequined his skin. She watched
until watching became indistinguishable from desire,

so when she laid herself on asphalt, in the back
where she hauled the trash at closing, it felt

inevitable, as if they were twins
who'd been severed by a scalpel.

Like every in Miami, that summer was hotter than hell.
The window AC, in the flat she'd rented on the beach,

rattled and leaked. One night she returned to find
roaches, the size of small rats, mating

in the kitchen sink. Fire extinguisher at hand,
she doused them and shuttered the kitchenette's accordion door.

Months later, after she'd quit the pub, he called
to say he'd been thinking of her and to read a poem.

Nobody not even the rain has such small hands,
he concluded. And she thought—

how could he know she'd been waiting
for someone to recite that one?—

a thought born of the yearning a young girl has
for her yearning to be real.

Each day but Sundays, that summer before,
she'd pulled double shifts to pay rent.

How many times, she can't recall, she'd come home late and sit
cross-legged on the futon, counting tips, rolling change.

How many times she watched the moon
dissolve into the sun—waiting for someone

to alter her short history of sex: power
and powerlessness—then dragged herself up to dress

and drive back across the Venetian Causeway.
On either side of the narrow road,

light spangled off the bay—
she'd been waiting for someone to make her believe

the self is not a mirage, not a dream the body dreams—
and she'd think: its surface is dazzling.

N°91
TRACI BRIMHALL

Unrequited Sublime in Three Notes

The first note comes postmarked from Tahiti,
climbing orchids pressed between the creases
of a letter that says, *Wait for me. I'll be home soon,*
in a rushed and heavy cursive you've never seen.
The middle note comes with tonka bean tea
in the envelope, and, *Drink this to chase away*
the ghost of my mistress, written on the flap you lick
to try and taste the mystery who loves you, whose
mistress starts to follow you down the streets,
pinches you while you sleep and asks, *Why you?*
Why you? You don't know but want to deserve
the love you've been given. You want its spirits,
its flora, its unsigned epistles. *Darling,* you say,
laughing at the jokes you think it might tell you.
Sweetheart, you say, when it accepts your offer
to give it the world or a minor constellation.
You see the moon at the bottom of your vodka,
but when you drink your way to it you find nothing
but the water-pocked coaster beneath your glass,
stained with the grays of lunar seas. *The heart is*
a homely hunter, you tell your friends, who say, *no,*
you mean lonely. Packaged with a mood ring bought
in a Miami airport and a Bergamot orange, the last
note reads, *Send me a Calabrian lemon, and I'll return,*
signed with the heart's oldest iamb, *my dear, my dear.*

N°92
JEHANNE DUBROW

The Long Deployment

For weeks, I breathe his body in the sheet
        and pillow. I lift a blanket to my face.
There's bitter incense paired with something sweet,
        like sandalwood left sitting in the heat
or cardamom rubbed on a piece of lace.
        For weeks, I breathe his body. In the sheet
I smell anise, the musk that we secrete
        with longing, leather and moss. I find a trace
of bitter incense paired with something sweet.
        Am I imagining the wet scent of peat
and cedar, oud, impossible to erase?
        For weeks, I breathe his body in the sheet—
crushed pepper—although perhaps discreet,
        difficult for someone else to place.
There's bitter incense paired with something sweet.
        With each deployment I become an aesthete
of smoke and oak. Patchouli fills the space
        for weeks. I breathe his body in the sheet
until he starts to fade, made incomplete,
        a bottle almost empty in its case.
There's bitter incense paired with something sweet.
        And then he's gone. Not even the conceit
of him remains, not the resinous base.
        For weeks, I breathed his body in the sheet.
He was bitter incense paired with something sweet.

N° 93
CHAD DAVIDSON

Frozen Music

If that's what architecture is, bent
from the inner workings of our ears,
some small stage around which windows
sizzle in rain; if what contains us

barely holds a fluster of wind over keys,
a few catgut strings and the guitarist
raising his difficult coda to the gel lights,
which almost float among the ficus;

if, given time, song hardens into girder;
if an auditorium's hum and pleasant dark
were darker yet when merely concretized,
then what to make of the pervading scent

that mischievous club gave off in Perugia,
all soft on the skin but barbed underneath,
a handful of forks under a napkin? Understand:
Italy, with its ardent terror for sweet

astringencies—vinegars disappearing
further in their tiny balsa, blood oranges
crying on a cutting board, all the monks
sealed in their humilities, reaping juniper

and sage for some elixir smoke-black
and metallic, like licking a lamppost
after rain—pleasure must first pass
through fire, must chafe and blister

and in doing so make its cure the joy.
Remember those lovers in the front row,
drinking in each other and the tune
we all had heard a hundred times?

And yet that time was different, if only
for the heavy drapes of it unfurling
around them in their private euphoria.
Different because that song was now theirs,

some small rented room with a boiler plate,
a fridge with a few wrinkled pears
inside, a Gorgonzola wedge, and, as often
happens in paradise, almonds

rusting in a glass dish atop the stereo,
on which plays that song, that song
that erected itself around them, that carried
an odor like money, on fingers, after it is spent.

N° 94
GREGORY FRASER

Balmy Accords

In the flower garden over cocktails she parsed the phrase
crime of passion, its ontology, she said, *strictly tautological.*

We stood beneath tupelo trees, gazing down a grassy
incline, beneath which spread a lake—darkened window

onto another lake. I was listening but also recollecting
my friend Homer, who once lived in Homer, New York,

where he taught the *Iliad* and *Odyssey* to farm kids,
and the chicken feathers I had witnessed on the drive

to her place, fluttering off an eighteen-wheeler packed
with cages, the white fluff like cottonwood seeds.

She sipped her drink and turned to cautions: *If we spend
our lives*, she said, *trying not to make enemies, we end*

with "husks of friends." I liked the thought and told her so,
told her she was on a roll, even with my doubts about

the cupidity with which she must have held the coinage
in mind, before delivering it with such an air of knowing.

Knowing. Air. Suddenly I had a mind to frame a tautology
of my own, but noticed with delight the way she lifted off

her garden hat and brushed back hair, revealing ears
like the tinted cantharus shells I had long ago admired

in a field guide, and wished one day to slip inside a poem—
as a hand might slip inside a fine silk blouse, or fine

perfume a fellow's nose (Ambre Précieux, say, with top
notes of lavender and myrrh, balmy accords)—a poem

not epic or heroic, of course. Unless such coy exchanges
in late spring under black gum trees, above a dark lake, are.

N°95
NED BALBO

Thinking of Coleridge's "This
Lime-tree Bower My Prison"

> *The first blast is a spicy lime with woody undertones.*
> —Online review of Tom Ford's scent Azure Lime

You make me think of blue skies, lime-tree bowers
in which Coleridge, imprisoned, found delight,
however far his friends or long the hours
he waited while they hiked the countryside.
Hobbled by boiled milk and heavy heart,
he focused on leaves and bees, not on his marriage
two years old, endangered from the start.
His friends, the wife who'd suffer a miscarriage
he visualized upon a hilltop heath,
transported; envious of all that touched
their eyes and memory, he ground his teeth,
determined to feel joy....
                              Alone, he watched
the radiant ivy, twilight turned to dark...
Your wood-notes: like a vanished lime-tree's bark.

N°96
REBECCA HAZELTON

But That Is No Indictment

The filthy cross
          between the barbershop slap
              of his face
         the distant vanilla of her mouth

   and a desire
        to please

once meant sailing away
on the deck of a pleasure boat
    festooned with gaudy lights

            where canopied revelers swung
                from arm to arm
           easy in the knowledge of deserved
                  happiness—

           but no one ever did
           stow away and wake up
           in the arms of a creamy heiress
               or stumble to shore
       to the banks of the Seine
              and vomit artistically
       with other expatriates —

Now a cashmere coat
        crumpled in the back of their shared closet
           rescued and rehung
     releases once more that scent

           only to suggest the swinging censers
              of religious
              pageantry

the incense that masks
        the accumulated stench of unwashed pilgrims
                of sacrifice

              rental agreements
                groceries
          the rules of monogamy
                or nearly

the acrid where to goes and what thens
    of which we make the future.

N° 97
KATY DIDDEN

After Ambre à Sade

Marquis de Sade, imprisoned
(for all he knew) for life, hung
tapestries over the walls
of his cell in the Bastille.
Lover of whips and fetters,
needing pain to feel pleasure,
imagine his ecstasy
gorging on ripe strawberries
like the damned outwitting hell—
that bass line's a tantric spell
in the perfume on my wrist.
Some claim that violence
can mark the spirit's resilience
or clarify one's essence.
I like humours more diffuse,
like the humor of the two
who mixed this scent—tempering fruit
and leather with patchouli—
one note of sweaty hippy
transforming vile de Sade into
Sade—the sweetest taboo.
Who prizes complexity?
O love, my muddled feelings—
I need you. I am afraid
to leave you. I've been waylaid
here in the dark wood of doubt,
searching for the next way out.
Now this strange spirit visits
me, a mingled composite
of cedar and tonka bean
that blends into my own skin
like some guide sent to pull me
beyond capability—
as if it will take both me
and more than me to match you,
some unlooked-for, external
grace to turn love eternal.

What mask will let my face show through?
What form free me to love you?

N°98
SETH ABRAMSON

Stockholm

There are tragedies downtown
the air of a little winter
        can catch. At the theater a man says
this is a tragedy
        and a woman says
I know. When a theater's empty you can do
        anything, the man says,
or say everything, he adds, and again she says
I know. But really

nobody talks like that. I once heard somebody
say in a theater
words that float down past the projector now
so I can begin
        my accounting of air. Because I believe
in honest capital.
        I believe when I return to the city
with the smell of Old Tjikko beneath my shoes

there's always at least one man underneath
the ground I stand on
        with the same parts I have,
one man travelling through the underground
thinking of the things he lives without
I live without also. Outside the theater above

I walk past a park and uphill and homeward
through a treeline
as he's whisked away on another line
        to whatever's next. They can't change
their fidelities, a man says,

        Or I can't, he adds,
then the lights lift everyone, a woman says
we'll see,
and the end of a line is just the part of a line
tragedies permit. I have two clean

pennies in my pocket, seven clean banknotes,
one clean sock, one clean ear,
sixteen clean nails, and everything else, I say,
      everything else.
I know, she says. And she does. We both do.

N° 99
IDRA NOVEY

At a Certain Point in a Marriage

Say a man enters and a woman leaves the room.
Say the man loves her but never says this.
Say the scent after she exits is tender
as a felled tree only the man can't tell
what the smell is. He thinks orchids or torn cloth,
maybe clouds. Say the woman pulls out her coat
and there it is again, her own perfume
and it's like smelling the heat lost
through large windows all winter.
Say the man follows her out to the hall.
Say he lifts her wrist to his mouth.

N° 100
ELANA BELL

Your Scent Does Not Remind Me…

Of the scent of the sea

Nor the dirt of an open field

Not of the narrow market alleys of old Jerusalem—
old men drinking coffee in doorways, the vegetables
displayed like jewels…

Not the bright sweet under the skin of a ripe peach
or the green of young sugarcane, fresh cut

Not milk from the goat whose name I whispered
each morning as I squeezed,
though she was not mine

She was not mine

Not my grandmother's kitchen
where borscht boiled on the stove
Or years later, the smell of her sweet breath
as she lingered before dying

Not the tender folds of the back of a baby's neck
or the smell of my fingers & hair after sex
Not the copper of my monthly blood

Nothing that comes from my body
Or the body of this earth

Though I once held a fine rose between my fingers
and crushed its petals for oil

Though I took its head in my mouth
and chewed until all that was left:

the smell of beauty on my breath
a few thorns pressed to my palm

CONTRIBUTORS' & MATCHMAKING NOTES

Seth Abramson is the author of three collections of poetry, most recently *Thievery* (University of Akron Press, 2013), winner of the 2012 Akron Poetry Prize, and *Northerners* (Western Michigan University Press, 2011), winner of the 2010 Green Rose Prize from New Issues Poetry & Prose. A graduate of Harvard Law School and the Iowa Writers' Workshop, he is currently a doctoral candidate in English literature at University of Wisconsin-Madison and the series co-editor for *Best American Experimental Writing* (Omnidawn, 2014). Links to his poems, poetry reviews, and essays on politics and popular culture can be found at sethabramson.net.
Seth Abramson was paired with the scent Umbra from Ramon Monegal.

Cristin O'Keefe Aptowicz is a poet and nonfiction writer. Her most recent awards include the ArtsEdge Residency at the University of Pennsylvania (2010-2011), a National Endowment for the Arts Fellowship in Poetry (2011), and the Amy Clampitt Residency (2013). Her sixth book of poetry, *The Year of No Mistakes*, was released by Write Bloody Publishing in Fall 2013, and her second book of nonfiction, *Dr Mütter's Marvels: A True Tale of Intrigue and Innovation at the Dawn of Modern Medicine*, will be released by Penguin's Gotham Books in Fall 2014. For more information, please visit her website: aptowicz.com
Cristin O'Keefe Aptowicz was paired with the scent New Haarlem from Bond No. 9.

James Arthur is the author of *Charms Against Lightning* (Copper Canyon Press, 2012). His poems have also appeared in *The New Yorker*, *The New Republic*, *Poetry*, *Ploughshares*, and *The American Poetry Review*. He has received a Hodder Fellowship, a Stegner Fellowship, the Amy Lowell Travelling Poetry Scholarship, a

"Discovery" / *The Nation* prize, and a residency at the Amy Clampitt House. He is an Assistant Professor at Johns Hopkins University, where he teaches in the Writing Seminars.
James Arthur was paired with the scent Grand Néroli from Atelier Cologne.

Sarah Arvio's latest book, *night thoughts: 70 dream poems & notes from an analysis* (Knopf, 2013) is a hybrid of poetry, prose, and memoir. Her earlier books are *Visits from the Seventh* (Knopf, 2002) and *Sono: cantos* (Knopf, 2006). She has won the Rome Prize, and Guggenheim and Bogliasco Fellowships, among other honors. For many years a translator for the United Nations in New York and Switzerland, she has also taught poetry at Princeton. A lifelong New Yorker, she now makes her home in Maryland near the Chesapeake Bay.
Sarah Arvio was paired with the scent Grapefruit from Jo Malone.

Beth Bachmann's first book, *Temper,* won the 2008 AWP Donald Hall Prize, published through the Pitt Poetry Series, and received the 2010 Kate Tufts Discovery Award. Her new manuscript, *Do Not Rise,* was chosen by Elizabeth Willis as winner of the 2011 Poetry Society of America's Alice Fay Di Castagnola Award.
Beth Bachmann was paired with the scent Narcisse Noir from Caron.

Aaron Baker's first collection of poems, *Mission Work* (Houghton Mifflin, 2008) won the Bakeless Prize in Poetry and the Glasgow/ Shenandoah Prize for Emerging Writers. A former Wallace Stegner Fellow in Poetry at Stanford University, he received his MFA in creative writing from the University of Virginia. He has been awarded fellowships by the Bread Loaf Writers' Conference and the Sewanee Writers' Conference, and has published work in numerous literary journals, including *Poetry, Virginia Quarterly Review, New England Review,* and *Post Road.* He is an Assistant Professor in the creative writing program at Loyola University Chicago.
Aaron Baker was paired with the scent Incense Rosé from Tauer.

Ned Balbo's third book, *The Trials of Edgar Poe and Other Poems* (Story Line Press, 2010), was selected for the Donald Justice Prize by A. E. Stallings and also awarded the 2012 Poets' Prize. *Lives of the Sleepers* (University of Notre Dame Press, 2005) received the Ernest Sandeen Prize and a *ForeWord* Book of the Year Gold Medal; *Galileo's Banquet* was awarded the Towson University Prize. He is co-winner of the 2013 Willis Barnstone Translation Prize and was featured poet in the Fall 2011/Winter 2012 *Valparaiso Poetry Review*. He lives in Baltimore with his wife, poet-essayist Jane Satterfield, and her daughter Catherine.
Ned Balbo was paired with the scent Azure Lime from Tom Ford.

Brian Barker is the author of *The Animal Gospels* (Tupelo Press, 2006) and *The Black Ocean* (SIU Press, 2011), winner of the Crab Orchard Open Competition. His poems, reviews, and interviews have appeared or are forthcoming in such journals as *Poetry, American Poetry Review, Kenyon Review Online, Indiana Review, Ploughshares, TriQuarterly, The Writer's Chronicle, The Washington Post, The Cincinnati Review, Blackbird,* and *Pleiades.* He teaches at the University of Colorado Denver.
Brian Barker was paired with the scent Black Violet from Tom Ford.

Rick Barot has published two books of poems with Sarabande Books: *The Darker Fall* (2002), and *Want* (2008), which was a finalist for a Lambda Literary Award and won the 2009 Grub Street Book Prize. He teaches at Pacific Lutheran University in Tacoma, WA, and in the low-residency MFA Program for Writers at Warren Wilson College.
Rick Barot was paired with the scent Orange Sanguine from Atelier Cologne.

Sandra Beasley is the author of *I Was the Jukebox*, winner of the Barnard Women Poets Prize, and *Theories of Falling*, winner of the New Issues Poetry Prize. Honors for her work include the Center

for Book Arts Chapbook Prize, the Lenoir-Rhyne University Writer-in-Residence position, the University of Mississippi Summer Poet in Residence position, two DCCAH Artist Fellowships, and the Maureen Egen Exchange Award from *Poets & Writers*. Her most recent book is *Don't Kill the Birthday Girl: Tales from an Allergic Life*, a memoir and cultural history of food allergy. She lives in Washington, D.C.
Sandra Beasley was paired with the scent Blackberry & Bay from Jo Malone.

Nicky Beer is the author of the book of poems *The Diminishing House*, which won the 2010 Colorado Book Award for poetry. Her awards include a grant from the National Endowment for the Arts, a Ruth Lilly Fellowship, a scholarship and fellowship from the Bread Loaf Writers' Conference, and a "Discovery" / *The Nation* award. She is an Assistant Professor at the University of Colorado Denver. She is fond of Olène by Diptyque and Rum Tonic by Malin+Goetz.
Nicky Beer was paired with the scent Beyond Love, By Kilian.

Erin Belieu is the author of four collections of poetry from Copper Canyon Press, including her latest *Slant Six* (2014).
Erin Belieu was paired with the scent English Pear & Freesia from Jo Malone.

Elana Bell's first collection of poetry, *Eyes, Stones* (LSU Press, 2012) was selected as the winner of the 2011 Walt Whitman Award from the Academy of American Poets. Her work has recently appeared in *AGNI, Harvard Review, Massachusetts Review*, and elsewhere. Elana leads creative writing workshops for women in prison, for educators, for high school students in Israel, Palestine, and throughout the five boroughs of New York City, as well as for the pioneering peace-building and leadership organization, *Seeds of Peace*. elanabell.com.
Elana Bell was paired with the scent Loukhoum from Keiko Mecheri.

Dan Bellm is a poet and translator living in Berkeley, California. The latest of his three books of poetry is *Practice* (Sixteen Rivers Press, 2008), winner of a 2009 California Book Award, and he has received fellowships from the National Endowment for the Arts and the California Arts Council. He translates poetry and fiction from Spanish and French, and teaches literary translation in the MFA in Creative Writing Program at Antioch University Los Angeles. danbellm.com.
Dan Bellm was paired with the scent Ambre Nue from Atelier Cologne.

Mark Bibbins is the author of three books of poems: *They Don't Kill You Because They're Hungry, They Kill You Because They're Full* and *The Dance of No Hard Feelings* (both from Copper Canyon Press), and the Lambda Award-winning *Sky Lounge*. He teaches in the graduate writing programs of The New School, where he co-founded *LIT* magazine, and Columbia University.
Mark Bibbins was paired with the scent Noir Epices from Editions de Parfums Frédéric Malle.

Mary Biddinger's most recent poetry collections are *Saint Monica* (Black Lawrence Press, 2011) and *O Holy Insurgency* (Black Lawrence Press, 2013). She is also co-editor of *The Monkey and the Wrench: Essays into Contemporary Poetics* (University of Akron Press, 2011). Her poems have appeared or are forthcoming in *Bat City Review, Crazyhorse, Crab Orchard Review, Guernica, Gulf Coast, Pleiades,* and *Sou'wester,* among others. She teaches literature and poetry writing at the University of Akron, where she edits *Barn Owl Review,* the Akron Series in Poetry, and the Akron Series in Contemporary Poetics.
Mary Biddinger was paired with the scent Spring Flower from Creed.

Traci Brimhall is the author of *Our Lady of the Ruins* (W.W. Norton, 2012), selected by Carolyn Forché for the 2011 Barnard Women Poets Prize, and *Rookery* (Southern Illinois University Press, 2010), winner of the 2009 Crab Orchard Series in Poetry First Book Award. Her poems have appeared in *Kenyon Review, Slate, The Believer, Ploughshares, New England Review, The New Yorker,* and *Best American Poetry 2013.* She has received fellowships from the Wisconsin Institute for Creative Writing, the King/Chávez/Parks Foundation, and the National Endowment for the Arts.

Traci Brimhall was paired with the scent Sublime Vanille from Creed.

Brian Brodeur is the author of the poetry collections *Natural Causes* (Autumn House Press, 2012), *Other Latitudes* (University of Akron Press, 2008), and the chapbook *So the Night Cannot Go on Without Us* (WECS Press, 2007). New poems and interviews are forthcoming in AWP's *The Writer's Chronicle, Shenandoah,* and *The Southern Review.* Brian curates the blog "How a Poem Happens," an online anthology of over 150 interviews with poets. He lives with his wife in Cincinnati where he is a George Elliston Fellow in Poetry in the PhD in English and Comparative Literature program at University of Cincinnati.

Brian Brodeur was paired with the scent Tuscan Leather from Tom Ford.

Jericho Brown is the recipient of fellowships from the Radcliffe Institute for Advanced Study at Harvard University and the National Endowment for the Arts. His poems have appeared or are forthcoming in journals and anthologies, including *Callaloo, The Nation, The New Yorker, Oxford American, The New Republic, 100 Best African American Poems, Ascent of Angles,* and *The Best American Poetry.* His first book, *Please,* won the American Book Award, and his second book, *The New Testament,* was published by Copper Canyon Press in 2014. Brown is currently an Assistant Professor at Emory University.

Jericho Brown was paired with the scent Spicebomb from Viktor&Rolf.

Michelle Chan Brown's *Double Agent* was the winner of the 2011 Kore First Book Award, judged by Bhanu Kapil. Her work has appeared or is forthcoming in *Blackbird, Cimarron Review, The*

Journal, The Missouri Review, Quarterly West, Sycamore Review, Witness, and others. A Kundiman fellow, Michelle received her MFA from the University of Michigan, where she was a Rackham Fellow. She was a Tennessee Williams scholar at the Sewanee Writers' Conference and received scholarships from the Vermont Studio Center and the Wesleyan Writers' Conference. Her chapbook, *The Clever Decoys*, is available from LATR Editions. She lives in DC, where she teaches, writes, and edits *Drunken Boat*.
Michelle Chan Brown was paired with the scent Peau de Pêche from Keiko Mecheri.

Stacey Lynn Brown is a poet, playwright, and essayist who received her MFA from the University of Oregon. Her work has appeared in numerous journals, including *Crab Orchard Review, Copper Nickel, Barn Owl Review, The Rumpus*, and *Poetry Daily*, as well as the *From the Fishouse* and *Southern Poetry* anthologies. She is the author of the book-length poem *Cradle Song* (C&R Press, 2009), and she is the co-editor, with Oliver de la Paz, of *A Face to Meet the Faces: An Anthology of Contemporary Persona Poetry* (University of Akron Press, 2012). She teaches at Indiana University in Bloomington.
Stacey Lynn Brown was paired with the scent Rose Anonyme from Atelier Cologne.

Lisa D. Chávez has published two books of poetry, *Destruction Bay* and *In an Angry Season*. Her essays have appeared in *Arts and Letters, The Fourth Genre*, and other magazines, and in anthologies including *The Other Latin@: Writing Against a Singular Identity*, and *An Angle of Vision: Women Writers on their Poor and Working Class Roots*. In addition to reading and writing, she has a keen interest in Japanese dogs and in perfume.
Lisa D. Chávez was paired with the scent Sanguine from Keiko Mecheri.

Chad Davidson is the author of *From the Fire Hills* (2014), *The Last Predicta* (2008), and *Consolation Miracle* (2003), all from Southern

Illinois University Press, as well as co-author with Gregory Fraser of *Analyze Anything: A Guide to Critical Reading and Writing* (Bloomsbury, 2012) and *Writing Poetry: Creative and Critical Approaches* (Palgrave Macmillan, 2009). He is a Professor of literature and creative writing at the University of West Georgia near Atlanta. *Chad Davidson was paired with the scent Les Nombres d'Or Vétyver from Mona di Orio.*

Erica Dawson's second collection of poems, *The Small Blades Hurt*, was published by Measure Press in January 2014. Her first collection, *Big-Eyed Afraid*, won the 2006 Anthony Hecht Prize and was published by Waywiser Press. Her poems have appeared in *Birmingham Poetry Review, Harvard Review, VQR, Best American Poetry 2008* and *2012*, and other journals and anthologies. She teaches at University of Tampa, in both the undergraduate English and Writing program and the MFA in Creative Writing Low-Residency program. *Erica Dawson was paired with the scent Red Roses from Jo Malone.*

Katy Didden has an MFA from the University of Maryland, and a PhD in English and creative writing from the University of Missouri. Her first book, *The Glacier's Wake*, won the 2012 Lena-Miles Wever Todd Prize from Pleiades Press. She is currently a Hodder Fellow at Princeton University. *Katy Didden was paired with the scent Ambre à Sade from Nez à Nez.*

Jehanne Dubrow is the author of four poetry collections, including most recently *Red Army Red* and *Stateside* (Northwestern University Press, 2012 and 2010). In 2015, University of New Mexico Press will publish her fifth book of poems, *The Arranged Marriage.* Her work has appeared in *New England Review, Ploughshares, Poetry, Prairie Schooner*, and *The Southern Review.* She is the Director of the Rose O'Neill Literary House and an Associate Professor of creative writing at Washington College. *Jehanne Dubrow was paired with the scent Incense Oud, By Kilian.*

Michael Dumanis is the author of the poetry collection *My Soviet Union* (University of Massachusetts Press, 2007), winner of the Juniper Prize for Poetry; and the co-editor of *Legitimate Dangers: American Poets of the New Century* (Sarabande, 2006) and *Russell Atkins: On the Life and Work of an American Master* (Pleiades Press, 2013). He teaches literature and creative writing at Bennington College.
Michael Dumanis was paired with the scent Bois Blonds from Atelier Cologne.

Moira Egan's most recent poetry collection is *Hot Flash Sonnets* (Passager Books, 2013). In 2014, Pequod will publish a bilingual volume, *Strange Botany/Botanica Arcana*. Her work has appeared in many journals and anthologies in the U.S. and abroad, and with her husband, Damiano Abeni, she has published more than a dozen books in translation in Italy. A long-term devotee of olfaction, Moira has recently begun to explore in her poems the various paradoxes of scent: its ephemeral nature vs. the deep-seated memories it can arouse in an instant, bypassing thought; and the challenge of rein-venting language to describe olfactory experiences.
Moira Egan was paired with the scent Mon Parfum Chéri, Par Camille from Annick Goutal.

Robin Ekiss is a recipient of a Rona Jaffe Award for emerging women writers and is a former Stegner Fellow in poetry at Stanford. Her book, *The Mansion of Happiness* (University of Georgia Press, VQR Poetry Series, 2009), won the 2010 Shenandoah/Glasgow Prize. She has received awards and residencies from the Bread Loaf Writers' Conference, Millay Colony for the Arts, MacDowell Colony, and Headlands Center for the Arts. Her poems have appeared in *The Atlantic Monthly, Poetry, APR, Kenyon Review, New England Review*, and elsewhere. She's a contributing editor for *ZYZZYVA* and on the Executive Committee of Litquake, the West Coast's largest literary festival.

Robin Ekiss was paired with the scent Petite Chérie from Annick Goutal.

Jill Alexander Essbaum is the author of several collections of poetry including *Harlot* (No Tell Books, 2007), *Necropolis* (NeoNuma Arts, 2009), and the single poem chapbook *The Devastation* (Cooper Dillon, 2010). She lives in Austin, TX.
Jill Alexander Essbaum was paired with the scent Sweet Oriental Dream from Montale.

Tarfia Faizullah is the author of *Seam* (SIU, 2014), winner of the Crab Orchard Series in Poetry First Book Award. Her poems appear in *American Poetry Review, Ploughshares, New England Review, Kenyon Review, Best New Poets 2014, The Missouri Review,* and elsewhere. Honors include fellowships and scholarships from Kundiman, the Fulbright Foundation, Bread Loaf, Sewanee, Kenyon Review Writers Workshop, and Vermont Studio Center. She is the Nicholas Delbanco Visiting Professor in Poetry at the University of Michigan Helen Zell Writers' Program.
Tarfia Faizullah was paired with the scent Jasmin Rouge from Tom Ford.

Elyse Fenton is the author of the poetry collection, *Clamor.* Her second manuscript won the 2013 Alice Fay Di Castagnola Award from the Poetry Society of America. She lives with her family in Portland, Oregon.
Elyse Fenton was paired with the scent Mistral Patchouli from Atelier Cologne.

Rebecca Morgan Frank is the author of *Little Murders Everywhere* (Salmon, 2012), a finalist for the Kate Tufts Discovery Award, and her poems have appeared such places as *Guernica, Ploughshares, The Missouri Review* online, *Verse Daily,* and *32 Poems.* She received the Poetry Society of America's 2010 Alice Fay Di Castagnola Award for her new manuscript-in-progress. She is editor-in-chief and co-founder of the online literary journal *Memorious.org* and

an Assistant Professor at the University of Southern Mississippi's Center for Writers.
Rebecca Morgan Frank was paired with the scent Acqua Fiorentina from Creed.

Gregory Fraser is the author of three poetry collections: *Strange Pietà, Answering the Ruins,* and *Designed for Flight* (Northwestern University Press, 2014). He is co-author, with Chad Davidson, of the textbooks *Writing Poetry* (Palgrave Macmillan, 2009) and *Analyze Anything: A Guide to Critical Reading and Writing* (Bloomsbury, 2012). His poems have appeared in *The Paris Review, The Southern Review,* and *The Gettysburg Review,* among others. The recipient of a grant from the NEA, Fraser teaches English and creative writing at the University of West Georgia.
Gregory Fraser was paired with the scent Ambre Précieux from Maître Parfumeur et Gantier.

Elisa Gabbert is the author of *The Self Unstable* (Black Ocean, 2013) and *The French Exit* (Birds LLC, 2010). She blogs at thefrenchexit. blogspot.com.
Elisa Gabbert was paired with the scent Rose Oud, By Kilian.

Jeannine Hall Gailey recently served as the poet laureate of Redmond, Washington and is the author of three books of poetry, *Becoming the Villainess, She Returns to the Floating World,* and *Unexplained Fevers.* She was a 2013 Jack Straw writer and volunteers for *Crab Creek Review.*
Jeannine Hall Gailey was paired with the scent Safran Troublant from L'Artisan Parfumeur.

John Gallaher is the author of, most recently, *Your Father on the Train of Ghosts* (with G. C. Waldrep). His next book, *In a Landscape,* will be out in September 2014. He co-edits *The Laurel Review* and lives in rural Missouri.

John Gallaher was paired with the scent Avignon from Comme des Garçons.

Melody S. Gee is the author of *Each Crumbling House* (Perugia Press, 2010). Her poems and essays have appeared recently in *Copper Nickel*, *Pilgrimage*, *Connotation Press*, *failbetter*, and *Boxcar Poetry Review*. She was a 2008 Kundiman Poetry Retreat Fellow, and currently teaches writing at St. Louis Community College. More information at melodygee.com.
Melody S. Gee was paired with the scent Genie des Bois from Keiko Mecheri.

Carmen Giménez Smith is the author of a memoir, *Bring Down the Little Birds*, four poetry collections—*Milk and Filth*; *Goodbye, Flicker*; *The City She Was*; and *Odalisque in Pieces*. She is the recipient of a 2011 American Book Award, the 2011 Juniper Prize for Poetry, and a 2011-2012 fellowship in creative nonfiction from the Howard Foundation. Formerly a Teaching-Writing Fellow at the Iowa Writers' Workshop, she now teaches in the creative writing programs at New Mexico State University, while serving as the editor-in-chief of the literary journal *Puerto del Sol* and the publisher of Noemi Press.
Carmen Giménez Smith was paired with the scent Damascena from Keiko Mecheri.

Juliana Gray is the author of two books of poetry. Her second collection, *Roleplay*, won the 2010 Orphic Prize and was recently published by Dream Horse Press. Recent poems have appeared in or are forthcoming from *River Styx*, *Measure*, *32 Poems*, *Blackbird*, and elsewhere. An Alabama native, she lives in western New York and is an Associate Professor of English at Alfred University.
Juliana Gray was paired with the scent Vanille Abricot from Comptoir Sud Pacifique.

George Green grew up in western Pennsylvania but has lived

for over thirty years in Manhattan's East Village. His poems have appeared in the anthologies *Poetry 180, 180 More Poems, The Best American Poetry 2005* and *2006, Bright Wings: An Illustrated Anthology of Poems about Birds,* and *The Swallow Anthology of New American Poets.* His book, *Lord Byron's Foot,* won the 2012 New Criterion Poetry Prize. He has received an award in literature from the American Academy of Arts and Letters. He teaches at Lehman College, CUNY, in the Bronx.
George Green was paired with the scent Cardinal from Heeley.

Rachel Hadas is Board of Governors Professor of English at the Newark campus of Rutgers University and the author of over fifteen books of poetry, essays, and translations. Her memoir of her husband's illness, *Strange Relation,* was published in 2011, and her latest book of poems, *The Golden Road,* in 2012. Her honors include a Guggenheim Fellowship in Poetry and an award in literature from the American Academy of Arts and Letters.
Rachel Hadas was paired with the scent Champaca Absolute from Tom Ford.

Meredith Davies Hadaway is the author of *Fishing Secrets of the Dead* (2005) and *The River is a Reason* (2011), both issued by Word Press. Her poems and reviews have recently appeared in *Alaska Quarterly Review, Nimrod, Cincinnati Review, Grey Sparrow,* and *Poetry International.* Her work has earned four Pushcart nominations as well as Honorable Mention for both the Robinson Jeffers Tor House Poetry Prize and New Millennium Writings Award. She is currently the Rose O'Neill Writer-in-Residence at Washington College.
Meredith Davies Hadaway was paired with the scent Osmanthe Yunnan from Hermès.

James Allen Hall's first book, *Now You're the Enemy,* won awards from the Lambda Literary Foundation, the Texas Institute of

Letters, and the Fellowship of Southern Writers. Recent poems have appeared in *New England Review, Poem-A-Day, The American Poetry Review, Bloom*, and *Best American Poetry 2012*. He was a 2011 recipient of fellowships in poetry from the National Endowment of the Arts and the New York Foundation for the Arts. He teaches creative writing and literature at Washington College.
James Allen Hall was paired with the scent Dark Purple from Montale.

Leslie Harrison is the author of *Displacement*, published by Houghton Mifflin Harcourt. She has been awarded scholarships and fellowships at the Sewanee Writers' Conference and the Bread Loaf Writers' Conference, and a fellowship in literature from the National Endowment for the Arts. Recent poems have appeared or are forthcoming from *Pleiades, Subtropics, The New Republic, The Kenyon Review, FIELD*, and elsewhere. She is Assistant Professor of poetry at Towson University where she also co-directs the Towson Literary Reading Series. She had (literally) never worn perfume before her sample arrived in the mail. Her website is leslie-harrison.com.
Leslie Harrison was paired with the scent Nectarine Blossom & Honey from Jo Malone.

Yona Harvey is a literary artist living in Pittsburgh, Pennsylvania, USA. She is the author of *Hemming the Water* (Four Way Books, 2013), winner of the Kate Tufts Discovery Award, 2014, Claremont Graduate University. She was the Rose O'Neill Literary House's 2013 Cave Canem Writer-in-Residence. Her website is yonaharvey.com.
Yona Harvey was paired with the scent Bahiana from Maître Parfumeur et Gantier.

K. A. Hays is the author of two books of poetry: *Early Creatures, Native Gods* (Carnegie Mellon, 2012) and *Dear Apocalypse* (2009). Her poems, fiction, and verse translations have appeared in *The Kenyon Review, Best American Poetry 2009* and *2011, American Poetry Review,*

Hudson Review, Gulf Coast, and elsewhere. As Visiting Assistant Professor at Bucknell, in 2014 she is directing the Bucknell Seminar for Younger Poets and serving as editor of *West Branch* magazine. *K. A. Hays was paired with the scent Wild Bluebell from Jo Malone.*

Rebecca Hazelton is the author of *Fair Copy* (Ohio State University Press, 2012), winner of the 2011 Ohio State University Press / *The Journal* Award in Poetry, and *Vow*, from Cleveland State University Press. She was the 2010-11 Jay C. and Ruth Halls Poetry Fellow at the University of Wisconsin-Madison Creative Writing Institute and winner of the "Discovery" / *Boston Review* 2012 Poetry Contest. Her poems have appeared or are forthcoming in *AGNI, The Southern Review, Best New Poets 2011, Best American Poetry 2013*, and *Poetry*. *Rebecca Hazelton was paired with the scent Ambre Narguilé from Hermès.*

H. L. Hix's recent books include a poetry collection, *As Much As, If Not More Than* (Etruscan Press, 2014); a translation, made with Jüri Talvet, of a selection of poems by the Estonian peasant poet Juhan Liiv (*Snow Drifts, I Sing*; Guernica Editions, 2013); an essay collection, *Lines of Inquiry* (Etruscan Press, 2011); and an anthology, *Made Priceless* (Serving House Books, 2012). His website is hlhix.com. *H. L. Hix was paired with the scent Five o'clock au gingembre from Serge Lutens.*

Carrie Jerrell is the author of *After the Revival*, 2008 winner of the Anthony Hecht Poetry Prize from Waywiser Press. Carrie received her MA from Johns Hopkins University and her PhD from Texas Tech University. She is an Assistant Professor at Murray State University in Murray, KY, where she also works as the Associate Director of the MFA program and the coordinator of undergraduate creative writing. *Carrie Jerrell was paired with the scent Ginger Lily from Providence Perfume Co.*

Laura Kasischke has published eight books of poetry and eight novels. She teaches at the University of Michigan.
Laura Kasischke was paired with the scent Trèfle Pur from Atelier Cologne.

Dore Kiesselbach studied poetry at Oberlin College and the University of Iowa then practiced public housing law in New York City for several years before refocusing on writing post-9/11. His first collection, *Salt Pier* (Pittsburgh, 2012), won the Agnes Lynch Starrett Prize and contains work awarded Britain's Bridport Prize. Magazine appearances include *AGNI, Antioch Review, Poetry,* and *Field.* He lives in Minneapolis.
Dore Kiesselbach was paired with the scent Dry Wood from Ramon Monegal.

Keetje Kuipers has been the Margery Davis Boyden Wilderness Writing Resident, a Wallace Stegner Fellow at Stanford University, and the Emerging Writer Lecturer at Gettysburg College. Her first book, *Beautiful in the Mouth,* won the A. Poulin, Jr. Prize from BOA Editions and was published in 2010. Her second book, *The Keys to the Jail,* was published by BOA Editions in 2014. Keetje is an Assistant Professor at Auburn University.
Keetje Kuipers was paired with the scent Peony & Blush Suede from Jo Malone.

Ilyse Kusnetz received her PhD in feminist and postcolonial British literature from the University of Edinburgh. Her poetry has appeared in *Crab Orchard Review, Cincinnati Review, Crazyhorse, Stone Canoe, Rattle, Atlanta Review, Cimarron Review, Connotation Press: an Online Artifact, Women's Voices for Change,* and other journals. Her chapbook *The Gravity of Falling* was published by La Vita Poetica Press (2006). She has published many reviews and essays on contemporary American and Scottish poetry, both in the United States and abroad, and she is book review editor at *The Florida Review.* Her first book, *Small Hours* (Truman State University Press,

2014), won the T. S. Eliot Prize, and she teaches at Valencia College. *Ilyse Kusnetz was paired with the scent Blue Amber from Montale.*

Deborah Landau is the author of *Orchidelirium* and *The Last Usable Hour.* A third collection of poems, *The Uses of the Body*, is forthcoming from Copper Canyon Press (2015). She directs the Creative Writing Program at New York University.
Deborah Landau was paired with the scent Roseberry from Les Parfums de Rosine.

Nick Lantz is the author of the poetry collections *We Don't Know We Don't Know, The Lightning That Strikes the Neighbors' House,* and *How to Dance as the Roof Caves In.* His poems have appeared in numerous journals and on the nationally syndicated radio program *The Writer's Almanac* with Garrison Keillor. He teaches creative writing at Tinker Mountain Writers' Workshop, Queens University's low-residency MFA, and at Sam Houston State University, where he is the poetry editor of the *Texas Review.*
Nick Lantz was paired with the scent Wall Street from Bond No. 9.

Dorothea Lasky is the author of *ROME* (W.W. Norton/Liveright, 2014) and *Thunderbird, Black Life,* and *AWE,* all out from Wave Books. She is also the co-editor of *Open the Door: How to Excite Young People About Poetry* (McSweeney's, 2012) and was a 2013 Bagley Wright Lecturer on Poetry. Currently, she is an Assistant Professor of poetry at Columbia University's School of the Arts and lives in New York City.
Dorothea Lasky was paired with the scent Liaisons Dangereuses, By Kilian.

Born in Kobe, Japan and raised in the Pacific Rim, **Mari L'Esperance** co-edited (with poet Tomás Q. Morín) the anthology of essays, *Coming Close: Forty Essays on Philip Levine* (Prairie Lights Books/University of Iowa Press, 2013). She is also the author of *The Darkened Temple*, which was awarded a Prairie Schooner Book

Prize in Poetry (University of Nebraska Press, 2008), and an earlier collection *Begin Here*, awarded a Sarasota Poetry Theatre Press Chapbook Prize. L'Esperance lives in the Los Angeles area, where she works as a Licensed Marriage and Family Therapist.
Mari L'Esperance was paired with the scent Umé from Keiko Mecheri.

Shara Lessley is the author of *Two-Headed Nightingale* (New Issues, 2012). A former Stegner Fellow at Stanford, her awards include an Artist Fellowship from the State of North Carolina, the Diane Middlebrook Fellowship from the Wisconsin Institute for Creative Writing, Colgate University's O'Connor Fellowship, The Gilman School's Tickner Fellowship, Washington College's Mary Wood Fellowship, and a "Discovery" / *The Nation* prize. Shara's poems have appeared in *Ploughshares, The Kenyon Review, The Southern Review, The Missouri Review,* and *New England Review,* among others. A recent resident of the Middle East, Shara is completing a new collection titled *The Explosive Expert's Wife.*
Shara Lessley was paired with the scent Roses Elixir from Montale.

Sandy Longhorn is the author of *The Girlhood Book of Prairie Myths*, winner of the 2013 Jacar Press Full Length Poetry Book Contest, and *Blood Almanac,* which won the Anhinga Prize for Poetry. New poems have appeared in *Crazyhorse, Hayden's Ferry Review, Hotel Amerika, North American Review,* and elsewhere. Longhorn teaches at Pulaski Technical College, where she directs the Big Rock Reading Series. In addition, she co-edits the online journal *Heron Tree,* is an Arkansas Arts Council Fellow, and blogs at *Myself the only Kangaroo among the Beauty.*
Sandy Longhorn was paired with the scent Oranges and Lemons Say the Bells of St. Clement's from Heeley.

dawn lonsinger is the author of *Whelm* (winner of the 2012 Idaho Prize in Poetry). Her poems and lyric essays have appeared in *American Poetry Review, Black Warrior Review, Colorado Review,*

Crazyhorse, Guernica, Indiana Review, Subtropics, Best New Poets 2010,
and elsewhere. She holds an MFA from Cornell University and a
PhD from the University of Utah, and is now teaching creative
writing, poetry & politics, and monstrosity in literature & film at
Muhlenberg College. A Pushcart nominee, she is the recipient of
a Fulbright Fellowship, four Dorothy Sargent Rosenberg Prizes,
Smartish Pace's Beullah Rose Poetry Prize, and the Scowcroft Prize
chosen by Lydia Yuknavitch.
dawn lonsinger was paired with the scent Love and Tears, By Kilian.

Lindsay Lusby's poems have appeared or are forthcoming in *Fairy
Tale Review, The Lumberyard, Sugar House Review, The Feminist Wire,
Midway Journal, wicked alice, decomP, The Doctor T.J. Eckleburg
Review,* and *The Coachella Review.* Her first chapbook *Imago* was
released in early 2014 by dancing girl press. She is the Assistant
Director of the Rose O'Neill Literary House at Washington College
in Chestertown, Maryland. She recently bought her first bottle of
designer perfume, Spring Flower from Creed.
*Lindsay Lusby was paired with the scent Lime Basil & Mandarin from
Jo Malone.*

Amit Majmudar's poetry has appeared in *The New Yorker, The
Atlantic Monthly,* two *Best American Poetry* anthologies, *The Best of
the Best American Poetry 1988-2012, Poetry,* and the *Norton Introduc-
tion to Literature.* His first poetry collection, *0', 0',* was released by
Northwestern in 2009; his second, *Heaven and Earth,* was awarded
the Donald Justice Prize for 2011. He has published two novels, *Par-
titions* and *The Abundance.* He is also a diagnostic nuclear radiologist.
Amit Majmudar was not paired with a scent.

David Mason's books include *The Country I Remember, Arrivals,
Ludlow: A Verse Novel, News from the Village,* and *The Scarlet Libretto.*
His new collection is *Sea Salt: Poems of a Decade, 2004-2014.* Editor
of several textbooks and anthologies, he serves as poet laureate of

Colorado and teaches at The Colorado College.
David Mason was paired with the scent Oolang Infini from Atelier Cologne.

Adrian Matejka is the author of *The Devil's Garden* (Alice James Books, 2003) and *Mixology* (Penguin Books, 2009), which was a winner of the 2008 National Poetry Series. *The Big Smoke*, his new collection about the boxer Jack Johnson, was published by Penguin in May 2013. He teaches in the MFA program at Indiana University in Bloomington.
Adrian Matejka was paired with the scent Santal Wood from Montale.

Jamaal May is from Detroit, MI where he taught poetry in public schools and worked as a freelance audio engineer. His first book, *Hum* (Alice James Books, 2013), received the American Library Association's Notable Book Award and an NAACP Image Award nomination. Other honors include the *Indiana Review* Prize, the Spirit of Detroit Award, the Stadler Fellowship, a Cave Canem Fellowship, the 2014-2016 Kenyon Review Fellowship, and the 2014 Cave Canem Residency at the Rose O'Neill Literary House. Jamaal's poems appear in such publications as *The New Republic*, *The Believer*, *Poetry*, *Ploughshares*, *NYTimes.com*, and *Best American Poetry 2014*. He co-directs the Organic Weapon Arts Chapbook and Video Series with Tarfia Faizullah.
Jamaal May was paired with the scent Nutmeg & Ginger from Jo Malone.

Originally from Jamaica, **Shara McCallum** is the author of four books: *The Face of Water: New and Selected Poems*; *This Strange Land*, a finalist for the 2012 OCM Bocas Prize for Caribbean Literature; *Song of Thieves*; and *The Water Between Us*, winner of the 1998 Agnes Lynch Starrett Prize for Poetry. Recognition for her work includes a 2013 Witter Bynner Fellowship from the Library of Congress and a 2011 National Endowment for the Arts Poetry Fellowship. Her poems have been published in journals, anthologies, and textbooks in the US, UK, Caribbean, Latin America, and Israel and have been translated into Spanish and Romanian. She directs the Stadler Center for Poetry and teaches at Bucknell University. *Shara McCallum was paired with the scent A Shot of Thai Lime Over Mango from Jo Loves.*

Shane McCrae is the author of *Mule, Blood, Forgiveness Forgiveness*, and three chapbooks—most recently, *Nonfiction*. His poems have appeared in *The Best American Poetry, American Poetry Review, Fence, Gulf Coast*, and elsewhere, and he has received a Whiting Writer's Award and a fellowship from the NEA. He teaches in the brief-residency MFA program at Spalding University.
Shane McCrae was paired with the scent Figuier from Heeley.

Erika Meitner is the author of four books of poems, including *Ideal Cities* (Harper Perennial, 2010), which was a 2009 National Poetry Series winner, and *Copia* (BOA Editions, 2014). Her work has appeared in *Best American Poetry 2011, Tin House, Ploughshares, Best African American Essays 2010, The New Republic, APR,* and elsewhere. She is currently an Associate Professor of English at Virginia Tech, where she teaches in the MFA program, and is online at erikameitner.com.
Erika Meitner was paired with the scent L'Etrog from Arquiste.

Philip Metres is the author of a number of books and chapbooks, including *A Concordance of Leaves* (Diode, 2013), *abu ghraib arias* (Flying Guillotine, 2011), *To See the Earth* (Cleveland State University Poetry Center, 2008), and *Behind the Lines: War Resistance Poetry on the American Homefront since 1941* (University of Iowa, 2007). His work has appeared in *Best American Poetry* and has garnered two NEA Fellowships, the Thomas J. Watson Fellowship, four Ohio Arts Council Grants, the Creative Workforce Fellowship, the Beatrice Hawley Award (for the forthcoming *Sand Opera*), the Anne Halley Prize, the Arab American Book Award, and the Cleveland Arts Prize.

He teaches literature and creative writing at John Carroll University in Cleveland, Ohio. See philipmetres.com and behindthelinespoetry.blogspot.com for more information.

Philip Metres was paired with the scent Entre Naranjos from Ramon Monegal.

Tyler Mills is the author of *Tongue Lyre* (Southern Illinois University Press, 2013), which won the 2011 Crab Orchard Series in Poetry First Book Award. Her poems have received awards from *Crab Orchard Review, Gulf Coast,* and *Third Coast,* and have appeared in *AGNI, Best New Poets, The Antioch Review, Georgia Review, TriQuarterly Online,* and elsewhere. A graduate of the University of Maryland (MFA, poetry), Tyler Mills is currently a PhD candidate in the Program for Writers at the University of Illinois-Chicago.

Tyler Mills was paired with the scent Le Speculoos from L'Antichambre.

Ander Monson is the author of six books, a website, chapbooks, and so forth.

Ander Monson was paired with the scent Little Italy from Bond No. 9.

Idra Novey is the author of *Exit, Civilian,* selected for the 2011 National Poetry Series and named a Best Book of 2012 by *Cold Front* and *The Volta.* Her first book, *The Next Country,* received the Kinereth Gensler Award from Alice James Books. Her poetry has been featured on NPR's *All Things Considered* and in *Poetry, Slate, American Poetry Review,* and elsewhere. She teaches in the Creative Writing Program at Princeton University.

Idra Novey was paired with the scent Batucada from L'Artisan Parfumeur.

Lisa Olstein is the author of three books of poems: *Radio Crackling, Radio Gone* (2006), winner of the Hayden Carruth Award; *Lost Alphabet* (2009), named a *Library Journal* Best Book of the Year; and *Little Stranger* (2013), a Lannan Literary Selection. She teaches in the MFA programs at the University of Texas at Austin.

Lisa Olstein was paired with the scent Mango Nectar from Jo Loves.

Alan Michael Parker is the author of seven collections of poems, including *Long Division* (Tupelo, 2012), finalist for the 2012 Rilke Prize and winner of the 2012 North Carolina Book Award in Poetry, and three novels, including *The Committee on Town Happiness* (Dzanc, 2014). His other honors include three Pushcart Prizes, the Fineline Prize, the 2013 Randall Jarrell Award, and the Lucille Medwick Award from the Poetry Society of America. He is the Douglas C. Houchens Professor of English at Davidson College, and teaches in the University of Tampa low-residency MFA program.
Alan Michael Parker was paired with the scent Vanille Absolu from Montale.

Nathaniel Perry is the author of *Nine Acres* (APR/Copper Canyon, 2011). He is the editor of *The Hampden-Sydney Poetry Review* and lives with his family in rural southside Virginia.
Nathaniel Perry was paired with the scent Oud Wood from Tom Ford.

Kiki Petrosino is the author of two poetry collections: *Hymn for the Black Terrific* (Sarabande, 2013) and *Fort Red Border* (Sarabande, 2009). She is an Assistant Professor of English at the University of Louisville, where she teaches creative writing.
Kiki Petrosino was paired with the scent Tabac Citron from Providence Perfume Co.

Emilia Phillips is the author of *Signaletics* (University of Akron Press, 2013) and two chapbooks, most recently *Bestiary of Gall* (Sundress Publications, 2013). Her poems appear in *AGNI*, *Green Mountains Review*, *The Kenyon Review*, *Narrative*, and elsewhere. She is the recipient of the 2012 Poetry Prize from *The Journal*; second place in *Narrative*'s 2012 30 Below Contest; and fellowships from the Bread Loaf Writers Conference, U.S. Poets in Mexico, Vermont Studio Center, and Virginia Commonwealth University where she received her MFA in 2012. She is the 2013–2014 Emerging Writer Lecturer at Gettysburg College.

Emilia Phillips was paired with the scent Divine Noir from Providence Perfume Co.

Patrick Phillips's third collection, *Elegy with a Broken Machine*, is forthcoming in 2015 from Alfred A. Knopf. He is a recent Guggenheim and NEA Fellow, and author of *Boy* and *Chattahoochee*, which won the Kate Tufts Discovery Award. He has also received a Pushcart Prize, the Lyric Poetry Award from the PSA, and *VQR*'s Emily Clark Balch Prize. His book of translations, *When We Leave Each Other: Selected Poems of Henrik Nordbrandt*, was published in 2013. He lives in Brooklyn and teaches at Drew University.

Patrick Phillips was paired with the scent Green Irish Tweed from Creed.

Jessica Piazza is the author of two poetry collections: *Interrobang* (Red Hen Press, 2013) and the chapbook *This is not a sky* (Black Lawrence Press, 2014). Born and raised in Brooklyn, she currently lives in Los Angeles where she earned a PhD in English literature & creative writing from the University of Southern California. She is a co-founder of *Bat City Review* and Gold Line Press, and a contributing editor at *The Offending Adam*. Learn more at jessicapiazza.com.

Jessica Piazza was paired with the scent Ophélia from Heeley.

John Poch is Professor of English at Texas Tech University. His most recent book of poems is *Dolls* (Orchises Press, 2009). He has published poems in *AGNI*, *Poetry*, *Southwest Review*, *Yale Review*, and many other journals.

John Poch was paired with the scent Italian Cypress from Tom Ford.

Hilda Raz is editor of the poetry series at University of New Mexico Press and the poetry editor for *BOSQUE* (the magazine). She is the author of seven books, the editor of five books, and the co-writer of a memoir, with Aaron Raz Link, *What Becomes You* (University of

Nebraska Press, 2008). She was the editor of *Prairie Schooner* and founding director of the *Prairie Schooner* Book Prizes. She is also a director of the Goucher College MFA in Creative Nonfiction, a past president of AWP, and is Luschei Professor of English, emerita, at the University of Nebraska where she taught in the PhD program. *Hilda Raz was paired with the scent Flower of Immortality, By Kilian.*

Brynn Saito is the author of *The Palace of Contemplating Departure*, winner of the Benjamin Saltman Poetry Award from Red Hen Press (2013). She also co-authored, with Traci Brimhall, *Bright Power, Dark Peace*, a chapbook of poetry from Diode Editions. Brynn's work has been anthologized by Helen Vendler and Ishmael Reed; it has also appeared in *Virginia Quarterly Review, Ninth Letter,* and *Pleiades.* She is the recipient of a Kundiman Asian American Poetry Fellowship, the Poets 11 Award from the San Francisco Public Library, and the Key West Literary Seminar's Scotti Merrill Memorial Award. Currently, Brynn lives in the Bay Area and teaches at California Institute of Integral Studies and Sofia University.
Brynn Saito was paired with the scent Santal Massoïa from Hermès.

Jane Satterfield is the author of three poetry books: *Her Familiars, Assignation at Vanishing Point,* and *Shepherdess with an Automatic,* as well as *Daughters of Empire: A Memoir of a Year in Britain and Beyond.* Her honors include a National Endowment for the Arts Fellowship in poetry, the Faulkner Society's Gold Medal for the Essay, the *Mslexia* Women's Poetry Prize, and *The Bellingham Review*'s 49th Parallel Poetry Prize, as well as residencies in poetry and nonfiction from the Virginia Center for the Creative Arts. Satterfield is literary editor for the *Journal of the Motherhood Initiative* and lives in Baltimore.
Jane Satterfield was paired with the scent Menthe Fraîche from Heeley.

Zach Savich is the author of three books of poetry, including *The Firestorm.* He teaches at the University of the Arts in Philadelphia.

Zach Savich was paired with the scent Santal Blush from Tom Ford.

Jason Schneiderman is a Professor of English at the Borough of Manhattan Community College. He is the author of two books of poems: *Sublimation Point* (Four Way Books, 2004) and *Striking Surface* (Ashland Poetry Press, 2010).
Jason Schneiderman was paired with the scent Jeux de peau from Serge Lutens.

Bruce Snider is the author of the poetry collections, *Paradise, Indiana*, winner of the Lena-Miles Wever Todd Poetry Prize, and *The Year We Studied Women*, winner of the Felix Pollak Prize in Poetry. His poems have appeared in the *Best American Poetry 2012, American Poetry Review, Poetry, Ploughshares*, and *Gettysburg Review*. A former Wallace Stegner Fellow and Jones Lecturer at Stanford University, he is currently an Assistant Professor at the University of San Francisco.
Bruce Snider was paired with the scent Andy Warhol from Bond No. 9.

Gabriel Spera's first book of poetry, *The Standing Wave* (HarperCollins, 2003), was a National Poetry Series selection and also received the Literary Book Award in Poetry from PEN USA-West. His second collection, *The Rigid Body* (Ashland Poetry Press, 2012), received the Richard Snyder Publication Prize. Additional honors include an NEA Fellowship and a COLA (City of Los Angeles) Fellowship. He lives in Los Angeles, but grew up in New Jersey, amid the odd constellation of L'Oreal, Revlon, and Rahway State Prison.
Gabriel Spera was paired with the scent Central Park from Bond No. 9.

Alison Stine is a writer, teacher, and performer. Author of the books *Wait* (University of Wisconsin Press, 2011), *Ohio Violence* (University of North Texas Press, 2009), and *Lot of My Sister* (Kent State University Press, 2001), she is a former Wallace Stegner Fellow at Stanford University. With writing published in *The Paris Review*,

The Kenyon Review, Tin House, The Huffington Post, and *The Nation*, among others, her awards include a Ruth Lilly Fellowship from the Poetry Foundation and the Brittingham Prize. A recipient of scholarships from the Bread Loaf Writers' Conference, she holds a BA from Denison University, an MFA from the University of Maryland, and a PhD from Ohio University.
Alison Stine was paired with the scent Rose Ikebana from Hermès.

Yerra Sugarman is the author of two poetry collections: *Forms of Gone* and *The Bag of Broken Glass*, both published by The Sheep Meadow Press. She was awarded a 2011 National Endowment for the Arts Fellowship for poetry, the 2005 PEN/Joyce Osterweil Poetry Award, a "Discovery" / *The Nation* Poetry Prize, and awards from the Poetry Society of America. Her poems, translations, and articles have appeared in *Prairie Schooner, The Nation, Another Chicago Magazine, Literary Imagination, Pleiades, The Massachusetts Review*, and *The Oxford Encyclopedia of American Literature*, among other publications. She is a PhD candidate in literature and creative writing at the University of Houston.
Yerra Sugarman was paired with the scent Sel Marin from Heeley.

Mathias Svalina is the author of three books, most recently *The Explosions* from Subito Press. He is an editor of Octopus Books. Big Lucks Press will release his book *Wastoid* in 2014.
Mathias Svalina was paired with the scent Tobacco Vanille from Tom Ford.

Matthew Thorburn is the author of three books of poems, most recently *This Time Tomorrow* (Waywiser Press, 2013). He lives and works in New York City.
Matthew Thorburn was paired with the scent Manhattan from Bond No. 9.

Maureen Thorson is the author of the poetry collections *My Resignation* (Shearsman Books, 2014) and *Applies to Oranges* (Ugly Duckling Presse, 2011). She is the poetry editor for *Open*

Letters Monthly and lives in Washington, DC. Visit her online at maureenthorson.com.

Maureen Thorson was paired with the scent Aqua Allegoria Pamplelune from Guerlain.

Brian Turner is the author of *Here, Bullet* and *Phantom Noise.* His poetry and essays have been published in *The New York Times, National Geographic, Poetry Daily, VQR, The Georgia Review,* and other journals. He received a USA Hillcrest Fellowship in Literature, an NEA Fellowship in poetry, the Amy Lowell Travelling Fellowship, the Poets' Prize, and a fellowship from the Lannan Foundation. His work has appeared on National Public Radio, the BBC, *Newshour* with Jim Lehrer, and *Weekend America,* among others. He teaches and is the Director of the low-residency MFA at Sierra Nevada College.

Brian Turner was paired with the scent Blue Amber from Montale.

Sarah Vap is the author of five collections of poetry; the most recent are *Arco Iris* (Saturnalia Books, 2012) and *End of a Sentimental Journey* (Noemi Press, 2013). She is a recipient of a 2013 National Endowment of the Arts Grant for literature.

Sarah Vap was paired with the scent Insolence from Guerlain.

Cody Walker is the author of *Shuffle and Breakdown* (Waywiser, 2008) and the co-editor of *Alive at the Center: An Anthology of Poems from the Pacific Northwest* (Ooligan, 2013). His work appears in *Parnassus, Slate, Salon, The Yale Review, The Common,* and *The Best American Poetry.* He lives in Ann Arbor, where he teaches English at the University of Michigan.

Cody Walker was paired with the scent Pure Oud, By Kilian.

Connie Wanek is the author of three books of poetry, most recently *On Speaking Terms* from Copper Canyon Press (2010). Her son made her a website: conniewanek.com. She lives north of Duluth,

Minnesota, where the dominant scents are those of white pines, balsam, and (in season) lilacs.

Connie Wanek was paired with the scent Rose de Siwa from Parfums MDCI.

Caki Wilkinson is the author of the poetry collection *Circles Where the Head Should Be*, which won the 2010 Vassar Miller Prize. Her second collection won the Lexi Rudnitsky/Editor's Choice Award from Persea Books and is forthcoming in 2014.

Caki Wilkinson was paired with the scent Rose Water & Vanilla from Jo Malone.

Catherine Wing's second collection of poems, *Gin & Bleach*, won the Linda Bruckheimer Series in Kentucky Literature from Sarabande Books in 2012. Her poems have been published in such journals as *Poetry, The Nation,* and *The New Republic,* featured on *The Writer's Almanac,* and included in *Best American Erotic Poems* and *Best American Poetry 2010.* She teaches English and poetry at Kent State University and serves as the general editor for the Wick Poetry Center's Ohio Chapbook Series.

Catherine Wing was paired with the scent Lipstick Rose from Editions de Parfums Frédéric Malle.

Matthew Zapruder is the author of four collections of poetry, most recently *Come On All You Ghosts* (Copper Canyon, 2010), a *New York Times* Notable Book of the Year, and *Sun Bear* (Copper Canyon, 2014). A member of the core faculty of the MFA program at Saint Mary's College, he is also a senior editor at Wave Books. He lives in Oakland, CA.

Matthew Zapruder was paired with the scent Philosykos from Diptyque.

ACKNOWLEDGMENTS

Although all of the poems included in *The Book of Scented Things* are new works created specifically for the anthology, we are grateful to these literary magazines and journals for publishing the following pieces:

"Fable" from *Kartika Review* (Issue 16: Fall 2013), copyright 2013 by Michelle Chan Brown, used by permission of author.

"The Long Deployment" from *Poem-A-Day* (December 20, 2013), copyright 2013 by Jehanne Dubrow, used by permission of the Academy of American Poets, poets.org.

"Prediction, *Hyacinthoides non-scripta*" from *32 Poems* (Issue 11.1: Spring 2013), copyright 2013 by K. A. Hays, used by permission of author.

"Antoinette" from *TYPO Magazine*, copyright 2014 by dawn lonsinger, used by permission of author.

"Per Fumum" from *Poetry* (February 2014), copyright 2014 by Jamaal May, used by permission of author.

"Poem for a Vial of Nameless Perfume" from *Massachusetts Review* (Spring 2014), copyright 2014 by Matthew Zapruder, used by permission of author.

The following poetry collections recently released by our contributors also included their perfumed poems: